Chemistry!
BEST
SCIENCE
PROJECTS

Water Science Fair Projects

Using Ice Cubes, Super Soakers, and Other Wet Stuff

Madeline Goodstein

Enslow Publishers, Inc.

40 Industrial Road   PO Box 38
Box 398   Aldershot
Berkeley Heights, NJ 07922   Hants GU12 6BP
USA   UK

http://www.enslow.com

T 4763

Library of Congress Cataloging-in-Publication Data

Goodstein, Madeline P.
    Water science fair projects using ice cubes, super soakers, and other wet stuff /
Madeline Goodstein.
        v. cm. — (Chemistry! best science projects)
    Includes bibliographical references and index.
    Contents: Water is a very good solvent — The three states of matter of water —
Surface tension, adhesion, and cohesion of liquid water — Chemical properties of water.
    ISBN 0-7660-2124-6 (hardcover)
    1. Water—Experiments—Juvenile literature. [1. Water—Experiments. 2.
Experiments.] I. Title. II. Series.
    QC145.24.G66 2004
    507'.8—dc21
                                                            2003008510

Printed in the United States of America

10 9 8 7 6 5 4 3 2

To Our Readers: We have done our best to make sure all Internet Addresses in this book
were active and appropriate when we went to press. However, the author and the publisher
have no control over and assume no liability for the material available on those Internet sites
or on other Web sites they may link to. Any comments or suggestions can be sent by e-mail
to comments@enslow.com or to the address on the back cover.

Illustration Credits: Tom LaBaff

Cover Illustration: © Corel Corporation

Contents

Introduction 5

1 *The Structure of Water* 11

   1.1   What Makes Up Water? 12

   1.2   Can You Bend a Falling Stream
        of Water? 17

   1.3   Solubility 22

   1.4   How Much Salt Can Water Hold? 29

2 *The Three States of Matter of Water* 32

   2.1   Colored Ice 33

   2.2   Molecules Are Always in Motion 36

   2.3   Why Can an Ice Cube Float
        in Water? 39

   2.4   Heating Ice 46

   2.5   Evaporation Removes Heat 50

   2.6   Water, Water in the Air 52

   2.7   Purification by Distillation 56

3 *Surface Tension, Adhesion, and
Cohesion of Liquid Water* 59

   3.1   How Many Drops of Water Can a
        Penny Hold on Its Surface? 60

3.2   Feeling the Force of Surface Tension   64

3.3   Cohesive Versus Adhesive Forces   66

3.4   Shape of Liquid-Solid Interface   68

3.5   Raindrops   72

3.6   How Do Soaps and Detergents Work? . . .   75

3.7   What Is a Soap Bubble?   79

3.8   Capillarity: Water Can Walk up
the Sides of a Tube   83

3.9   Paper Chromatography   88

4   *Chemical Properties of Water*   93

4.1   Water Reacts With Metal Oxides   95

4.2   Does Iron React With Water?   98

4.3   Water Makes Some Reactions Possible . . .   100

4.4   Acids, Bases, and Indicators   103

4.5   Do Acids and Bases Neutralize
Each Other?   109

4.6   How Powerful Are the Hydrogen Ions? . .   113

4.7   Testing the Quality of Drinking Water. . . .   119

Glossary   123

*Further Reading and
Internet Addresses*   126

Index   127

Introduction

When you think of water, what comes to mind? It might be a glass of water, a stream, a pond, a lake, a sea, an ocean, or maybe rain, hail, snow, or floods. Imagine feeling thirsty, dry, parched, wet, soaked; showering, bathing, swimming, sailing, laundering, cooking, washing. Gurgling brooks, graceful fountains, thundering waterfalls, floating icebergs, creeping glaciers—all contain water.

Water is the most ordinary material in our lives, and it is the most extraordinary. It is different from all other materials. Water is the only substance that exists naturally on Earth in all three states of matter, as solid ice, as liquid water, and as a gas in the air. It is different from all other substances in its structure, in its uses, in its behaviors. It makes up almost three quarters of the weight of our bodies, and we cannot live without it.

Water shapes our land. It cuts gorges, eats away at coastlines, creates caves, makes deserts and lakes, and carries stones and rocks in its streams and huge boulders in its glaciers. It helps to steer our weather, engaging in a gigantic cycle. Water evaporates into the skies, condenses into clouds and rain, flows over and under the surface of the earth, and evaporates back into the skies.

Civilizations have flourished where water was plentiful, proud empires have been destroyed by lack of water, and wars have been fought over the rights to water. Today, polluted waters are a major concern of all nations.

What is this mighty substance? Water is not a single element but a compound made up of two elements: hydrogen and oxygen. Its physical and chemical properties are often strikingly different from those expected based on the behaviors of other liquids. This book will delve into the chemistry of water to explore how and why it is so unusual.

EXPERIMENTS AND PROJECTS

Many special properties of water will be examined through experiments. This book will walk you through dozens, but you will also be given many suggestions for independent investigations and for science fair projects that you can do yourself. All the materials needed for the experiments and projects are available in your home or in a local supermarket, hardware store, or drugstore. The experiments are fun and easy to do. They are safe to carry out when the instructions are properly followed. Consult with your school science teacher or other responsible adult to obtain approval before starting any experiments of your own.

All data (observations) that you collect should be written in your science notebook. The notebook should be bound so that you have a permanent record. Be sure to include the date, experiment number, and a brief description of how you collected the data.

There are now some excellent books available on how to prepare a display for a science fair, and you should consult them.

Projects about chemistry have special needs with respect to displays. You cannot show the chemical changes as they take place. Instead, photograph or draw them. Many chemical changes are colorful, so use color to make pictures more striking. Show the materials used at the start of the reaction and those produced at the end of the reaction by enclosing them in containers such as sealed petri dishes or plastic bags that you mount on a display. Photograph or draw any special laboratory tools and the laboratory apparatus you set up. Be inventive about different ways of showing what took place.

SCIENTIFIC PROCESS

A scientific experiment starts when someone wonders what would happen if a certain change were made. Suppose you gradually added salt to water until no more salt dissolved. What would happen if the saltwater were then cooled? A guess about what would happen is called a hypothesis. The hypothesis might be that additional salt could be dissolved in the cooler water. Another hypothesis might be that some of the dissolved salt would come back out of the water. Perhaps there would be no change in the quantity of the salt in the water. You can do an experiment to find out whether your hypothesis is correct.

A scientific experiment has only two variables in it, that is, only two things that can change. For the saltwater experiment, you would change one variable, the temperature, and the result would be a change (perhaps) in the other variable, the quantity of salt dissolved in the water. Nothing else may change—not the amount of water, the purity of the water, or even the kind of container that is used. If anything else were allowed to change, it would not be possible to tell which variable had caused the change in the solubility of the salt. Your hypothesis, procedure, data, and conclusions should all be recorded in your science notebook.

Suppose you carried out the saltwater experiment and found no change in the quantity of salt dissolved when it cooled. This would not mean that the experiment was a failure. It provided useful information. Other ideas can then be explored, such as what happens when the saltwater is further cooled or what happens when it is heated. In the same way, you may wish to explore other ideas for scientific experiments based upon what you find by doing the experiments in this book.

Logical explanations may be offered to explain the observed behaviors. These explanations are called theories and must be tested by further experimentation. If scientists find that the evidence from experiments provides compelling support for the theory, the theory is accepted. But scientists are careful about accepting new theories. If any of the experimental evidence contradicts a theory, then the theory must be discarded or altered. That is the scientific process.

SAFETY

Experimenting with chemicals can be dangerous unless certain precautions are taken. It is your responsibility to use all the chemicals only as directed in this book. The precautions necessary to prevent accidents and to make the experiments safe and enjoyable are easy to follow.

- ✓ Never taste any materials listed in this book unless specifically directed to do so. Never put your fingers to your mouth while working on an experiment.

- ✓ Always wash your hands with warm water and soap after an experiment. Also, wash the surfaces on which you have carried out the experiment.

- ✓ Wear goggles (safety glasses) in experiments as directed. All chemists wear goggles when working in the laboratory. Goggles can be purchased in hardware or dollar stores.

- ✓ Be sure to have an adult supervise your work or do part of it when the directions call for it.

- ✓ When using certain solvents, adequate ventilation, such as an exhaust fan or an open window, is necessary.

- ✓ Some solvents are flammable and should not be used near a flame.

- ✓ Wear plastic gloves when handling chemicals. The thin disposable gloves that may be used on either hand and are sold in packs of about one hundred in dollar stores or hardware stores are very convenient for this purpose.

- ✓ Some chemicals should not be flushed down the sink or thrown into the garbage. Instructions will be given for disposal of such materials in an experiment.

Consideration must always be given to safety when working with chemicals. Therefore, it is essential that **all investigations and science fair projects be approved by a responsible adult**. Where warranted, the experimentation should take place under adult supervision. If there are any questions about safety, the adult should be sure to obtain the approval of a science teacher before allowing the experiments.

It is a good idea to wear an apron and to work on surfaces that can take water damage. Covering a surface with newspapers or plastic sheeting will help to protect it.

You should use purified water for experiments unless otherwise stated. Distilled or deionized water sold at the supermarket may be used for this purpose. Natural water from a spring or other sources may be safe to drink but is not considered pure because it contains dissolved solids.

And now, on to the experiments!

Chapter 1

The Structure of Water

In one drop of water are found
all the secrets of the universe.
— *Kahlil Gibran, poet*

The oceans contain almost all of the water on Earth. But ocean water has too much salt in it to be drinkable. Why is the ocean salty? Where does the salt come from?

The answer has to do with the geological cycle of water on our Earth. As rainwater trickles down from the surface, it dissolves some of the salt that lies naturally in the ground. The water drains into brooks, streams, and rivers until it cascades into the oceans. There, the dissolved solids (salts) stay, but some of the water evaporates. From the clouds that form, rain falls to the ground, and the cycle is repeated. As a result, some salt always remains in the oceans. There are certain beaches where stranded piles of salt crystals may be found. They are the result of pools of ocean water that evaporated back into the skies until only dry salt was left.

Experiment 1.1

What Makes Up Water?

Materials

- ✓ safety goggles
- ✓ 9-volt battery
- ✓ battery cap for 9-volt battery or two copper wires
- ✓ scissors or knife
- ✓ drinking glass
- ✓ tap water
- ✓ teaspoon
- ✓ vinegar
- ✓ **an adult**

Put on your safety goggles. Attach a battery cap with its two dangling wires to a 9-volt battery. If you do not have a battery cap, you can attach a copper wire about 15 cm (6 in) long to one of the two battery terminals and another similar length of copper wire to the other terminal. Before attaching the wires, **have an adult** cut away any insulation that covers both ends of the wires so that at least 1 cm (½ in) of copper is exposed on each. Fill a drinking glass with tap water and add about a teaspoon of vinegar. Allow the free ends of the two battery wires to dip into the water without touching each other, as shown in Figure 1. What do you observe?

Did you see a small stream of bubbles emerging from the ends of each wire? The electric current broke down the water into the two chemical elements from which it is made. One of the elements bubbles off as a gas at one wire, and the other bubbles off at the other wire. Hydrogen is flammable, so remove the battery after a brief observation and disconnect the wires.

The chemical formula of water is H_2O. This formula shows that each separate particle of water is made of two atoms of hydrogen, H (the subscript 2 indicates that there are two atoms

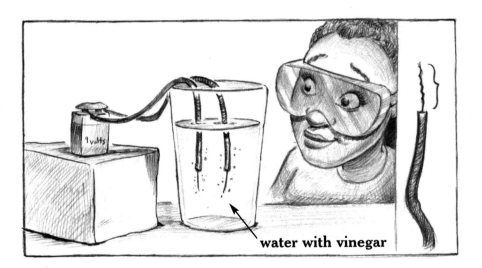

water with vinegar

Figure 1.

ELECTROLYSIS OF WATER

Electricity is passed from a 9-volt battery through two copper wires into impure tap water. The water is decomposed into two gases. One gas bubbles off the end of one wire, and the other bubbles off the end of the other wire.

of H) and one atom of oxygen, O. Note that when there is only one atom of a chemical element in a formula, the subscript 1 is left out of the formula. Just one spoonful of water contains over a trillion trillion water particles, each made up of two atoms of hydrogen and one of oxygen. The smallest particle of any pure material that can exist independently is called a molecule, so each H_2O particle is a molecule of water.

Figure 2 shows how the three atoms in a water molecule are arranged. Each atom is represented by a circle. Each straight line between atoms represents the chemical bond that ties the atoms to each other. The lines may be drawn to any length; they represent only the bond, not the distance between the atoms. As shown in Figure 2, water is a bent molecule, where the oxygen atom is connected to two hydrogen atoms to form an angle of 104.5 degrees.

Based on the formula of water, what were the gases that appeared at each wire?

Energy is needed to break water into its two elements. The battery supplies electrical energy to do this. The process of supplying electrical energy to cause a chemical change is called electrolysis. The reaction that was caused by electrical energy is shown below in simplest form in chemical shorthand.

$$2\,H_2O \rightarrow 2\,H_2 + O_2$$

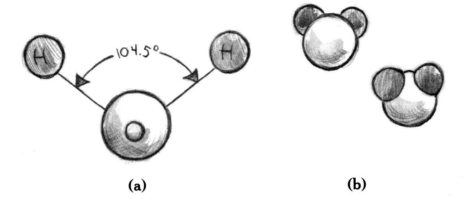

(a)   (b)

Figure 2.

STRUCTURE OF A WATER MOLECULE

a) The bent structure is shown by lines representing the bonds that connect the oxygen atom to the two hydrogen atoms at an angle of 104.5 degrees.

b) Another way of depicting a water molecule is shown in two different views. In each, the larger circle represents an oxygen atom and the two smaller circles the hydrogen atoms. The view at the left shows the oxygen atom at the top of the water molecule, with two hydrogen atoms below. At the right, the water molecule is shown from the other side, with the two hydrogen atoms on top and the oxygen atom below.

A more descriptive shorthand is shown below followed by the same reaction in words.

$$2 \text{ H}_2\text{O } (l) + \text{energy} \rightarrow 2 \text{ H}_2 (g) + \text{O}_2 (g)$$
water (liquid) and energy   yield   hydrogen (gas) and oxygen (gas)

Science Project Idea

Pure water does not conduct electricity and so cannot undergo electrolysis. That was why a little vinegar had to be added to the water in Experiment 1.1. You can use this knowledge to test for purity of water. Is your tap water pure? If you filter the tap water through a cartridge, is the filtered water pure? Test bottled deionized (or distilled) water from the supermarket, and test bottled spring water. If you have stream or pond water, test these, too. Do you think ocean water will conduct electricity? If you can obtain a sample, try that. If not, you can simulate ocean water by adding some salt to tap water. What other waters can you test? Did you find any pure water?

Experiment 1.2

Can You Bend a Falling Stream of Water?

Materials

✓ sink

✓ nylon comb

✓ salt, sugar, artificial sweetener, cornflakes, paper, and Styrofoam

✓ tabletop

All atoms are made up of combinations of particles called protons, electrons, and neutrons. Protons and neutrons exist in the tiny central core, or nucleus, of the atom. Electrons orbit the nucleus a minute distance away. The space occupied by an orbiting electron or group of electrons is called the shell. Table 1 shows the charges and locations in the atom of the particles that make up an atom.

Table 1.

PARTICLES IN AN ATOM

Name	Electrical Charge	Location
electron	negative	shell
proton	positive	nucleus
neutron	none	nucleus

The charge on one proton equals the charge on one electron. An atom is neutral when it has an equal number of positive and negative charges. Is it possible to show that there are charged particles in atoms using only simple household materials?

Turn on the faucet to produce a thin stream of water. Run a nylon comb several times through your hair. Slowly move the teeth of the comb toward the stream, as shown in Figure 3. How close does the comb get before you see a change in the stream? What do you observe? Bring the comb a little closer. Does this increase the effect?

Figure 3.

A nylon comb is gradually brought closer to a thin falling stream of water.

Did you see the stream bend toward the comb? The drops in the stream of water are attracted to the charged comb even though the comb never touches them. What causes the stream of water to bend?

When you combed your hair, some electrons jumped from either your hair to the comb or from the comb to your hair. Which way electrons jump depends on what the rubbed materials are made of. As was shown in Table 1, electrons are the carriers of negative electrical charge. So, the material that gains the electrons becomes negatively charged. The material that loses the electrons becomes positively charged. Electrical charge accumulated on an object in this way is called static electricity.

It is a rule of nature that the same kinds of charges (like charges) repel each other, but unlike charges attract each other.

When water falls in a stream, the stream is made up of tiny droplets of water. The molecules in these droplets gather some static electricity as they fall. Let's say that the comb has gained negative static electricity. As a result, the comb attracts positive charge and repels negative charge on the water. The protons in the water move toward the comb, and the electrons move away. Since the protons are closer, their attractive forces are stronger. This attraction makes the lightweight droplet move toward the comb.

When you run a nylon comb through your hair, both the comb and your hair become charged. Other plastics used to make combs or rulers or other shapes may also produce this effect.

Try using a charged comb to see if it can attract neutral lightweight objects. Place small samples of material spread out on a tabletop and hold the comb horizontally above them. For samples, consider solids such as salt, granulated or powdered sugar, and artificial sweetener, and bits of cornflakes, paper, and Styrofoam. What happens? Do your results support the idea that matter is electrical in nature?

The neutral objects that you just tested have an equal number of positive and negative charges in them. Only the electrons in matter can move around in response to outside charge. When a charged object is moved near neutral objects, it may cause a temporary redistribution of charge within the molecules of the object. If the object is lightweight enough, the force of electrical attraction can be sufficient to overcome gravity so that the particles move toward the charged object.

With the stream of water, it is believed that the large bending effect observed is due primarily to the static electricity that accumulates on the falling drops. The static electricity responds to the charged comb. Additional bending is contributed by the effect of the charged comb on neutral water molecules.

Science Project Ideas

- Try rubbing other solid materials such as glass or Styrofoam to see if they accumulate enough charge to deflect a falling stream of water. Also rub the solids with different materials such as acrylic, silk, or wool. Which produces the most bending? Which produces the least?

- Experiment to find whether there is an object that can be charged so as to deflect a stream of water away from it. Explain your findings.

Experiment 1.3

Solubility

Materials

- ✓ measuring cup
- ✓ purified water
- ✓ small clear drinking glasses or jars
- ✓ plastic or stainless steel spoons
- ✓ teaspoon
- ✓ tablespoon
- ✓ eyedropper
- ✓ Epsom salts (hydrated magnesium sulfate)
- ✓ ground pepper
- ✓ candle wax
- ✓ small chunk of Styrofoam or plastic wrap
- ✓ sugar
- ✓ baking soda (sodium bicarbonate)
- ✓ rubbing alcohol (isopropyl alcohol 90% or higher)
- ✓ cooking oil (such as olive, corn, or canola oil)
- ✓ mineral oil
- ✓ sink

When a little table salt is stirred into water, the salt disappears. It is somewhere in the water, but it can no longer be seen. This is the property of solubility. The salt has dissolved into the water; the water acts as a solvent. Are all materials soluble in water?

The nine solids and liquids listed after *eyedropper* in the above materials list are likely to be found in your home. Samples of each material will be tested for solubility in water. Which do you think are insoluble (do not dissolve) in water? Which do you think are only slightly soluble (only a pinch or so dissolves) in water? Which substances do you think are moderately soluble? Are there any solids that are very soluble or any liquids that are completely miscible (disappear into it no matter how much you add) with water?

Table 2 shows a sample chart for recording the data in this experiment. Copy it into your science notebook to use for this experiment.

Table 2.

SOLUBILITIES OF COMMON HOUSEHOLD MATERIALS

Name of Material	Solid or liquid	Solubility					Comments
		None	Slight	Moderate	High	Miscible	
Epsom salt	solid						
ground pepper	solid						
candle wax	solid						
plastic wrap	solid						
sugar	solid						
baking soda	solid						
rubbing alcohol	liquid						
cooking oil	liquid						
mineral oil	liquid						

Place ¼ cup of purified water (described in the last section of the Introduction) into a clear jar or glass. Use a clean, dry spoon to obtain a sample of Epsom salts about the size of a rice grain. Drop the Epsom salts into the water. Stir for about thirty seconds. After stirring, observe what happens to the sample. If the sample is still there after stirring, it is insoluble. No further testing of the sample is needed. If the sample disappears, go on to the next step.

Add a level teaspoon of Epsom salts to the jar already containing dissolved Epsom salts in water. Stir again for about one minute. Do all of the Epsom salts disappear? If the sample does not dissolve, then it is only slightly soluble in water and no further test is needed. If it disappears, go on to the next step. If it disappears, does the water look different than it did before?

For the next step, add 2 tablespoons of the Epsom salts to the jar already containing Epsom salts in water. Stir well for at least a minute. If the solid disappears, the Epsom salts are highly soluble. Otherwise, the Epsom salts were moderately soluble.

Repeat this same procedure separately for ground pepper, candle wax, a small chunk of Styrofoam or plastic wrap, sugar, and baking soda. When you are finished, throw the insoluble solids into the trash can. Pour used water solutions down the sink and flush with water.

Most liquids in the home are water solutions. Three liquids that are not water-based and that are safe for you to use are rubbing alcohol (isopropyl alcohol 90% or higher), cooking oil, and mineral oil. Place ¼ cup of purified water into a jar. Using a clean, dry eyedropper, add one drop of rubbing alcohol to the water. Stir vigorously. After stirring, observe what happens to the rubbing alcohol. If the alcohol is still there, either rising to float on top or sinking below the water, it is insoluble. No further testing is needed. If the alcohol disappears, it is at least slightly soluble. Go on to the next step.

Add a level teaspoon of the rubbing alcohol to the jar already containing a bit of it in water. Stir again for about a minute. Does the sample disappear? If it does not dissolve, then it is only slightly soluble in water and no further testing is needed. If it disappears, go on to the next step. If it disappears, does the water look different than it did before?

Next, add 2 tablespoons of the rubbing alcohol to the jar already containing rubbing alcohol in water. Stir well. If the alcohol disappears, it is completely miscible with water. Otherwise, the alcohol was moderately soluble.

Carry out the same procedure for cooking oil and mineral oil. Pour used liquids down the sink and flush with water.

What did you find out?

Why does water dissolve some substances and not others? The accepted explanation has to do with the polarity of the water molecules. As noted in Experiment 1.1, a water molecule is made up of two atoms of hydrogen and one of oxygen arranged so that the molecule is bent.

Because of the angle, as well as the elements that make it up, water is a polar molecule. A polar molecule is a molecule that is neutral overall, but the charges within it are unevenly distributed. There is an excess of negative charge on one side and a corresponding deficiency of negative charge on its other side. Oxygen atoms attract electrons much more strongly than hydrogen atoms do. As a result, the oxygen atom in water partially pulls the electrons away from the two hydrogen atoms, making the oxygen end more negative. Each hydrogen atom has only one proton and one electron. When its lone electron is pulled partially away, the proton that is left is partially exposed, making that side of the water molecule more positive. The result is a polar molecule in which the hydrogen ends are partially positive while the oxygen end is partially negative (see Figure 4).

Suppose water molecules were not bent but had atoms in a straight line. Would they be polar in that case? The answer is no.

Figure 4.

Water molecules are polar. Each has partial negative charge (δ^-) at the oxygen end of the molecule and partial positive charge (δ^+) at the hydrogen ends. A molecule is polar when it has a structure with an uneven distribution of charge.

There would be no excess of charge on one side of the molecule compared to the other. Each end would be alike in the distribution of charge. The bent structure makes the difference.

As noted earlier, unlike electrical charges—positive and negative—attract each other, but like charges—positive and positive or negative and negative—repel each other. This affects what happens when a polar molecule approaches another one. Molecules in the liquid state are continually moving around and can be attracted or repelled by nearby charges.

Figure 5 shows a diagram of water molecules near each other in liquid water. Notice how the polarity affects how they arrange themselves. The partially negative end of one molecule attracts the partially positive end of another and repels the negative end. The molecules are aligned accordingly.

A polar molecule dissolved in water is shown in Figure 6. Each water molecule around the polar molecule swivels so that

Figure 5.

A group of water molecules in the liquid state. Water molecules move so that, as much as possible, the partially positive end of one molecule points to the partially negative end of another molecule.

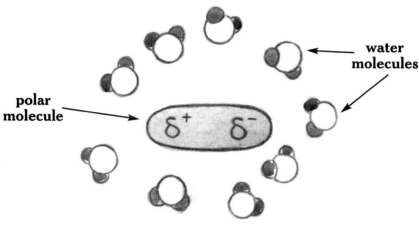

Figure 6.

A POLAR MOLECULE IN WATER

A polar molecule in water is shown with water molecules clustered around it. A water molecule approaching the negative end of a polar molecule turns so that its positive side faces that negative end. Similarly, a water molecule approaching the positive end of the polar molecule turns so that its negative side faces the positive end. As a result, the polar molecule develops a protective envelope of water molecules, which enables it to move freely around in the water.

it faces the opposite charge on the solute molecule. The polar molecule becomes surrounded by an envelope of water. This protective envelope enables it to move freely around in the water. As a result, the substance of which it is a part dissolves.

Nonpolar molecules cannot force their way into water. They cannot attract water molecules to form a protective envelope. As a result, substances with nonpolar molecules are unable to dissolve.

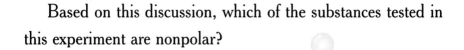

Based on this discussion, which of the substances tested in this experiment are nonpolar?

Experiment 1.4

How Much Salt Can Water Hold?

Materials

- ✓ measuring cup, at least 120 mL (4 oz)
- ✓ clear drinking glass
- ✓ purified water
- ✓ plastic wrap
- ✓ rubber band
- ✓ 2 stainless steel or plastic teaspoons
- ✓ table salt
- ✓ small clean, dry metal pot
- ✓ stove or other device to heat the water to boiling
- ✓ **an adult**

Is there a limit to how much salt can be dissolved in water?

Add 120 mL (4 oz) of purified water to a clear drinking glass. Cover the glass with plastic wrap, and secure the wrap with a rubber band. Allow the water to stand for about 20 minutes to allow it to reach room temperature. Remove the covering.

Add a level teaspoon of table salt to the water. Stir with a different teaspoon for a minute or two. Does all of the salt dissolve? If the added salt has completely dissolved, use the same dry spoon to keep adding teaspoons of salt while stirring with the other spoon until no more salt dissolves. At that point, the water is saturated with salt. Keep count of the teaspoons added. When no more salt dissolves, the solution is saturated with salt. How many teaspoons of salt dissolved in the 120 mL of water? One teaspoonful of table salt weighs about 4.5 grams. What was the mass of the dissolved salt?

To get the salt back, try boiling off the water. **Have an adult** do this as follows. Pour all of the salt solution into a small metal pot. Using the stove or other heating unit, boil the water until the pot is almost dry, but **never** boil it until dry. Remove the pot from the heat and allow it to stand until all of the remaining water evaporates into the air.

Does the solid in the dry pot look like the salt you had added? Taste a bit of it to see if it is salty. How many teaspoons of solid are in the pot? How does it compare to the number of teaspoons of salt that you put into the water? You may have to crush the solid to compare its measurement to that of the salt added to the water. What are your conclusions?

You can expect to find that when a substance dissolves in water, it does not react to become something else. It is still there and can often be recovered by boiling off the water.

Science Project Ideas

○ If you dry your tongue as much as possible, does salt placed on it taste salty? Find out. Suggest an explanation for your results. Repeat with table sugar.

○ An easy but lengthy way to get rid of water in a solution is to let the solution stand in an open container. The water will gradually evaporate, leaving the dissolved solid behind. Does salt obtained by this method look different than salt obtained by boiling off the water? Why?

○ Experiment to find out whether sugar dissolves in a solution that is saturated with salt. If so, how much dissolves? Is the quantity the same as when no salt is present? Will salt dissolve in a saturated sugar solution? Is the quantity that dissolves the same as when there is no sugar present?

○ When the temperature of the water is increased, does this change the quantity of table salt that dissolves? Find out. Repeat for sugar, baking soda, and other soluble household solids. Is there a rule that can be made, based on this limited evidence, about solubility and temperature?

Chapter 2

The Three States of Matter of Water

We call our home Earth—but
Water would be more apt.
—*Philip Ball, physicist and author*

About two thirds of the surface of our planet is covered by water. All that water causes our planet to look blue, an entrancing sight when viewed by astronauts in outer space. Graceful white swirls of clouds can be seen cutting across the blue. The whiteness is due to the tiny droplets of water that make up the clouds. Invisible gaseous molecules of water are also in the clouds.

Water is the only substance that has its own name, ice, for the solid state. About one twentieth of Earth's surface is covered by ice. The solid state of water has many variations of form. The Inuits are noted for an entire vocabulary of words used just to describe different forms of snow, among which are *saluma roaq* (fine smooth snow), *siqoqtoaq* (crusty top snow), *upsik* (wind-beaten snow), and *siqoq* (drifting snow).

This chapter will explore water's three states of matter.

Experiment 2.1

Colored Ice

Materials

✓ purified water   ✓ spoon
✓ small paper cup   ✓ freezer
✓ dark food coloring

Colored ice can yield a great deal of information about how water freezes. Fill a paper cup about halfway with purified water. Add two drops of dark food coloring. Stir well with a spoon. Place the cup in a freezer. How will the color be distributed in the ice?

When completely frozen, tear the paper cup off the ice. How is the color distributed? What is the shape of the color? How do you explain the location of the color?

The distribution of the color has to do with the way water freezes. Pure water freezes at 0°C (32°F). At the freezing point, ice crystals start to form first on the top of the water, where it is most exposed to the cold. Then the water freezes layer by layer until it is all solid. The freezing takes place all the way through the water in a definite crystalline pattern, invisible to our eyes. The pattern that water molecules form in ice is hexagonal (six-sided), with one water molecule occupying each of the six corners (see Figure 7). The hexagons are repeated like the cells in a honeycomb. Each layer of ice becomes a template for the water molecules in the next layer, which fit the same pattern.

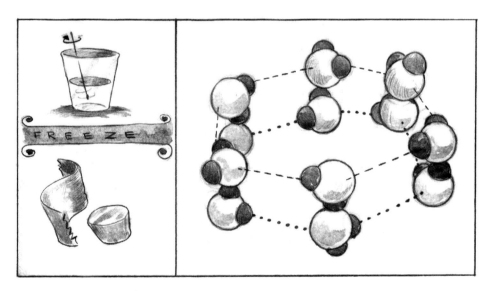

Figure 7.

THE MOLECULAR STRUCTURE OF ICE

Water molecules in ordinary ice are arranged in hexagonal layers like a honeycomb. To help distinguish between layers in this drawing, there are dashed lines between the molecules in the upper layer and dotted lines in the lower layer.

As a result, the hexagons form columns with empty centers. The food coloring that was added to the water is an impurity. It does not have the same shape as water and does not fit into the hexagonal pattern. As the ice forms, it pushes away the food coloring molecules. Eventually, as less and less water remains liquid, the coloring molecules remain trapped in the ice. As a result, the color appears mostly in the last sections to freeze. Does this agree with your observations?

Science Project Ideas

- How do ice machines make snow? Which kind of flakes do they make? How do they get powdered snow, the most desirable for skiing? Construct a miniature hand-operated snow machine. Describe your procedure. What kind of flakes do you get?

- Can a snowflake be preserved so that it can be exhibited? Invent a process for doing this. How well does your process work?

Experiment 2.2

Molecules Are Always in Motion

Materials

- ✓ glass jar
- ✓ water
- ✓ eyedropper
- ✓ dark ink or food coloring
- ✓ perfume or fresh bottle of ammonia
- ✓ **an adult**

When you look at a bowl of undisturbed water, no motion is visible. An ice cube in a freezer is motionless as long as you leave it alone, and water in the air does not seem to be hopping around the skies by itself. They all seem still—but they are not.

To see this motion indirectly, fill a jar with water and let it stand undisturbed for a while. With an eyedropper, allow one drop of dark ink or dark food coloring to enter the water at the top (see Figure 8). Carefully observe what happens. Is what happens due to gravity? Is it due to something else?

You will observe that the drop begins to sink. At the same time, it starts to break apart. Some of it sinks in swirls, while parts sink down or move sideways. Eventually the drop becomes completely spread out so that it darkens all of the water.

It is indeed gravity that pulls the drop downward. If there were no other forces acting, the drop would sink straight down. However, the drop keeps spreading out in many directions.

Figure 8.

A drop of dark ink falls in a jar of water.

This is because all the molecules that make up the colored drop are moving around, and so are all the molecules of water. The molecules of the colored drop hit moving molecules of water and are pushed around. After a while, all the molecules are so intermixed that you can no longer see the color separately.

Have an adult stand at least four feet away from you and open up a bottle of perfume or ammonia. How long does it take before you can smell it? The bottle should then be recapped.

You are only able to smell the odor if molecules of the perfume or ammonia reach your nose. What does the time it takes to smell it tell you about the molecules of gas that come out of the bottle? What does it tell you about the air?

It takes very little time to detect the smell from an open bottle even from across a room. Evidently, the odorous gas that escapes from the bottle moves very rapidly through the air to you. This suggests that molecules of gas also move around.

Based on observations like those you made in this experiment, scientists agree that the molecules of matter in all three states are all in motion. (See Figure 9 for diagrams of matter in the three physical states.) For water, molecules of water vapor are

Solid   Liquid   Gas

Figure 9.

PARTICLES IN THE THREE STATES OF MATTER

moving all the time, slamming into each other and into air molecules, then bouncing away again. Molecules of water in the liquid state are slithering around each other in all directions throughout the entire liquid. Even the particles of a solid are moving, but they just jiggle around in place, never changing places with the other particles of the solid. All particles in the three states are in motion.

Will the temperature of the water affect the movements of the coloring molecules? Find out by comparing the behaviors of a colored drop added to containers of hot water and of cold water. Do you think particles of matter move faster or slower as the temperature increases?

Experiment 2.3

Why Can an Ice Cube Float in Water?

Materials

✓ plastic container with tight cap

✓ tap water

✓ ice cube made from purified water

✓ freezer

Most liquids shrink when they freeze. Since the same mass of liquid occupies less space when frozen, it is denser as a solid than as a liquid. Water is different. Fill a hard plastic container with water to the top and cover it with a tight-fitting cap. Put the container in the freezer and leave it overnight to freeze. The next day, examine it. What changes have occurred? Does water shrink or expand on freezing?

Like other liquids, liquid water shrinks when cooled. Unlike other liquids, when water reaches the temperature of 4°C (39°F), a strange thing happens. As the water is cooled down further, it starts to expand and continues expanding until it freezes. As a result, ice takes up more space than the same water does as a liquid.

Will an ice cube float in water? Try it.

What causes water to freeze differently from all other liquids? The answer is hydrogen bonding.

Recall from Experiment 1.3 that water is a polar molecule. The oxygen end is partially negative while the hydrogen ends are partially positive. A hydrogen atom, even though bonded to its own oxygen atom, will also be attracted to the oxygen atom of any nearby water molecule. When close enough to the oxygen atom in another water molecule, the attraction is strong enough that the hydrogen forms a temporary bond with it. Such bonds are called hydrogen bonds. Figure 10 shows a hydrogen bond between two molecules of water.

A hydrogen bond between molecules is only about one-twentieth as strong as the bond between hydrogen and oxygen

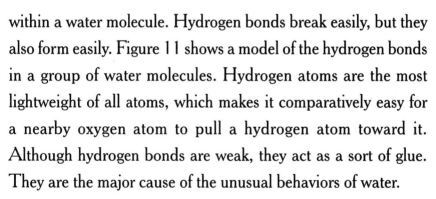

Figure 10.

A HYDROGEN BOND BETWEEN TWO MOLECULES OF WATER

The partially positive hydrogen atom of one water molecule has formed a temporary bond with the partially negative oxygen atom of a nearby water molecule.

within a water molecule. Hydrogen bonds break easily, but they also form easily. Figure 11 shows a model of the hydrogen bonds in a group of water molecules. Hydrogen atoms are the most lightweight of all atoms, which makes it comparatively easy for a nearby oxygen atom to pull a hydrogen atom toward it. Although hydrogen bonds are weak, they act as a sort of glue. They are the major cause of the unusual behaviors of water.

Molecules of matter move more rapidly as temperature increases and slow down as the temperature decreases. When molecular motion slows at lower temperatures, molecules bump less vigorously. As a result, they get closer to each other. However, at 4°C (39°F), the hydrogen bonds in liquid water start to keep the molecules from getting any closer to each other. As the temperature is lowered and the effect increases, the water

Figure 11.

Hydrogen bonds in liquid water cause a temporary chain of water molecules to form. The hydrogen bonds may form different types of temporary groupings, such as branched groups or three-dimensional groups.

expands. The expansion continues until the water freezes. It is the hydrogen bonding that is largely responsible for the honeycomb structure of ice (see Experiment 2.1) and for the spaces within the columns. Figure 12 shows how the hydrogen bonds hold ice in its hexagonal structure. If you will look at Figure 7 again, you will see that the dotted and dashed lines that were inserted to mark the two layers in the ice crystal also represent hydrogen bonds. Because of the effects of hydrogen bonding, water is denser than ice.

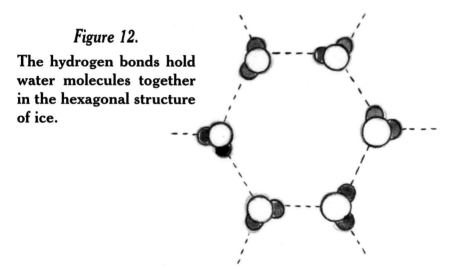

Figure 12.

The hydrogen bonds hold water molecules together in the hexagonal structure of ice.

If you froze 10 cups of water, how many cups of ice would you have?

Water expands by 10 percent when it freezes to ice. You would end up with 11 cups of ice. Eleven cups of ice in the space that had been occupied by 10 cups of water would shatter a cast iron pipe that is a foot thick. This has tremendous consequences for our Earth. Ice forces crevices apart and breaks stones and large rocks. It is a major cause of erosion of mountains.

The ice floating on lakes and ponds insulates the water below from further freezing. Because of this, life can continue under the ice. If ice sank into water, frozen water would fill lakes and oceans from the bottom up until they were all solid. Life as we know it would not be able to survive.

Science Project Ideas

- Look around your home for liquids that freeze at a temperature obtained in a freezer. For each, determine whether the solid sinks or floats as it is melted. What is the rule? Discuss the process and note how water is different. Use models or diagrams to show your results.

- Many people believe that when an ice cube is floating in a glass filled with water, the water will overflow as the ice melts. Develop an experiment to test this hypothesis.

- Devise an experiment to show that water expands 10 percent on freezing.

- The *Titanic*, considered an unsinkable ship when it was designed, sank on April 14, 1912, after it struck an iceberg.

The iceberg sliced open 200 feet along the side. Make a miniature iceberg using purified water (glaciers are made of rain water). You will need saltwater to mimic ocean water. Take measurements to find out how much of the iceberg's volume is above the saltwater and how much below. How much weight is that for each part? Draw or photograph the floating iceberg for your display. Discuss the consequences for the *Titanic*.

Does ice sink in alcohol? Investigate. Be sure to keep the isopropyl alcohol at a temperature below the freezing point of water. Isopropyl alcohol is sold in supermarkets and drugstores with differing percentages of water in it. Does the amount of water in the alcohol make a difference? What do the results tell about the densities of the materials?

Experiment 2.4

Heating Ice

Materials

✓ metal pot

✓ ice cubes made from purified water

✓ candy thermometer

✓ stove burner or other source of heat

✓ spoon

✓ safety goggles

✓ **an adult**

✓ clock or watch with second hand

Suppose you have a bowl of water at room temperature. You add some ice cubes and stir until the ice cubes have just about stopped melting. What is the temperature of the ice? Do you think that the temperature of the water is 0°C (32°F), or do you think that it is higher?

To find out, start by filling a metal pot with ice cubes made from purified water. Carefully insert a candy thermometer into the pot so that it is surrounded by ice, as shown in Figure 13. The thermometer should not touch the bottom of the pot. What is the temperature of the ice water? **An adult** should supervise the remainder of this experiment. Put on safety goggles. Turn the burner on the stove to low heat. If the burner is electric, allow a few minutes for it to warm up. Leave the burner on this setting for the remainder of the experiment.

Figure 13.

The time to melt ice and the temperature during melting are measured. When all the ice is melted, the time needed to bring the water to 10°C is measured.

If the thermometer reading is not at 0°C (32°F), wait until it is. Place the pot on the stove. Note the time in minutes and seconds that you did this. When the ice starts to melt, keep circulating the water gently with a spoon. Note the temperature of the water and the time when the ice starts to melt, after much of it has melted, after there is only a bit of ice left, and after all the ice is gone.

Allow the water to continue to heat after the ice is gone, stirring it occasionally. How long does it take to reach 10°C (50°F)? Which takes longer—to melt all the ice or to raise its temperature by 10°C? Make a graph of your data with the time on the x (horizontal) axis and the temperature on the y (vertical) axis. Use the graph to find out how long it would take to raise the temperature from 0°C to 100°C (212°F). How does the time compare with the time needed to melt all the ice?

What happens to all the heat that is added before the temperature starts to rise in the pot?

The answer is that the heat energy needed for melting goes to break the hydrogen bonds and polar attractions between ice molecules. These attractions hold the water molecules in the rigid crystalline ice structure. As long as any ice is present, the temperature of the water remains at 0°C. Once the ice structure is completely broken apart, the heat is needed mostly to speed up the motion of the molecules. The increasing speed is shown by the increasing temperature of the water.

Because of the hydrogen bonding, the heat needed to melt ice is greater than that needed to melt solids made from other liquids.

When there is a sudden increase in the temperature of the air, the vast oceans of water absorb the heat and become a little warmer. Conversely, if the air becomes suddenly cooler, the water cools a little and prevents a sharper drop. If the temperature drops to freezing, much heat is released when ice forms. This helps to prevent further temperature decrease. These reactions help to protect life in the environment and to modify wide swings in temperature during seasonal changes.

Science Project Ideas

What is the lowest temperature to which ice can be cooled in your home freezer? Find out what the temperature of the ice is in the butcher's freezer in your local store. Can you find a way to lower the temperature of ice even more? Do you think that there is a limit to how low the temperature of ice can sink?

When does water at a high temperature cool most rapidly, during the first minute of cooling or during a later one? Why?

Experiment 2.5

Evaporation Removes Heat

Materials

✓ damp cloth

✓ pot of purified water

✓ source of heat to boil water

✓ safety goggles

✓ **an adult**

✓ candy thermometer that reads above 100°C (212°F) and has a clip on it

✓ watch or clock with second hand

Use a damp cloth to lightly wet the back of your hand, then blow on your hand. What happens to the water? How does your hand feel?

Did you find that your hand felt cooler as it dried? The water evaporated (changed from liquid to gas) when you blew on it. The heat needed to evaporate the water was taken from your hand. Similarly, perspiration seeps out of the pores in your skin in hot weather to cool your body by evaporation. Evaporation removes heat from your body. Water is especially efficient at cooling because it absorbs more heat when it evaporates than do most other liquids.

When liquid water is heated to boiling and changes to a gas, does the temperature stay the same or gradually increase as the water is boiled out? If the heat is turned up higher, does that cause the temperature to rise? What are your predictions?

You can carry out the following experiment **under adult supervision** to answer the above two questions. Wear safety goggles during the experiment. You will need a pot of purified water, a source of heat, and a candy thermometer that can be read to above the boiling point of water. **Never allow a pot to be boiled dry**.

Fill the pot about halfway with purified water. Clip the candy thermometer to the inside of the pot so that the tip is immersed in the water but is not touching the pot. Note the temperature of the water. Start heating the water at a gradual but steady pace. Write down the temperature every half minute from the start. When the water starts to boil, continue heating for about 3 minutes and note the temperature every half minute.

Graph your data showing time on the x axis and temperature on the y axis.

What did you find out? Did it agree with your predictions? How does the graph show what happened?

The heat that is added to water to make it boil is used to tug apart molecules in the liquid state so that they are free to move off into the air. A good portion of the sun's energy is used to evaporate water from oceans, rivers, and lakes. The evaporation cools Earth, helping to keep it from being overwhelmed by the heat from the sun.

Science Project Idea

Why do many cake mix boxes provide different instructions for high-altitude baking? Investigate and explain. Provide exhibits of the product baked at high altitude compared to one baked at sea level to illustrate your explanation.

Experiment 2.6

Water, Water in the Air

Materials
- ✓ empty, clean, shiny metal can
- ✓ tap water
- ✓ freezer
- ✓ cereal bowl

Have you ever seen gaseous water? The answer has to be no. All gases are invisible. You may have seen droplets of steam in the air or droplets of your breath on a cold day, but these droplets are liquids, not gases. Is there water in the gaseous state in our air?

Fill an empty, clean, shiny metal can with tap water to about 2.5 cm (1 in) below the top. Place it into a freezer until the water is completely frozen. Remove the can from the freezer and put it, open end up, into a cereal bowl. Let it stand for a little while. What do you observe?

Soon, water moistens the side of the container. After a while, drops roll down the side into the bowl (see Figure 14). What is the source of this water? How much water can you collect?

Figure 14.

Water drops appear all around the outside of a can filled solidly with ice. The can is sitting at room temperature in a bowl, which will catch the drops as they fall.

The water that appears on the side of the can is coming from the air. Water is in the air all the time as a gas, completely transparent, invisible in the same way that air is invisible. When the water in the air encounters the ice-cold sides of the metal can, the water cools and condenses (changes from gas to liquid) onto the sides. Even in the dry air of an air-conditioned room, 5 mL of water (almost a teaspoon) can be collected within two hours by this method. In a warm, humid room, 10 mL can be collected over two hours by this method.

Other familiar examples of condensation include the water drops on cold-water pipes, water that is collected in air-conditioners and dehumidifiers, and early morning dew.

You might think that clouds are examples of water in the air as a gas. Since gases are invisible except for color, you are seeing droplets, not gaseous water. A single drop of rain may be made up of a million cloud droplets.

Science Project Ideas

- Use the method of Experiment 2.6 to compare the quantity of water in the air for the same length of time in each of the following situations:

a) in a bathroom before the tub is filled with room-temperature water and afterwards. Does filling the tub cause the air to contain more water? Discuss.

b) in a bathroom before the tub is filled with hot water and afterwards. Explain your observations.

c) in a room with no air-conditioning when the room is cold and when it is warmer.

For each of the above, state what might cause the amount collected to be elevated or lowered due to variables beyond your control.

In the method of Experiment 2.6, water may condense out of the air onto the icy sides of the can, but it may also evaporate back into the air from the bowl. Invent a way to collect the water without losing it to evaporation. Then, make additional explorations about the variables that affect condensation. Be sure to try to keep all variables constant except the one you are examining.

Compare the quantity of water that a dehumidifier in the home withdraws from the air in the summer to that in the winter.

How long can water be collected from the air using the method of Experiment 2.6, adding ice to the can as needed? Does the quantity collected constantly increase, or does it begin to decrease or even to remain the same? Explain.

Experiment 2.7

Purification by Distillation

Materials

✓ 3-qt glass, steel, or enameled pot (not aluminum or cast iron) with lid that has a handle on top at the middle

✓ 4-oz heat-resistant (Pyrex) pudding cup

✓ pieces of tile, slate, or flat stone that fit in the pot

✓ safety goggles, 2 pair

✓ **an adult**

✓ tap water

✓ dark food coloring

✓ stove or other source of heat

✓ tray of ice cubes

✓ several pot holders

✓ sink

One way to produce purified water is through the process of distillation. First, the water is boiled away. Impurities that boil above the temperature of water are left behind. The trick is to catch the boiled water while it is a gas, then cool it back to the liquid state.

An adult must supervise this experiment. Place a 3-qt pot on the burner, uncovered. A platform at least 3 cm (1 in) high is needed to support a cup inside the pot. The platform can be made of pieces of tile, slate, or flat stone piled up on each other (see Figure 15). Add enough cold sink water to the pot to come a little below the top of the platform. Add about four drops of dark food coloring to the water. Place a 4-oz heat-resistant (Pyrex) pudding cup on the platform. Put the lid on the pot

Figure 15.

**You can purify water by distillation
using simple home equipment.**

upside down. The knob or handle in the center of the lid should
be pointing to the pudding cup without touching it. Place 5 to 6
ice cubes into the lid. Put on your safety goggles. Turn on the
heat under the pot to a middle setting. After a while, the water
will start to boil and steam will be seen coming out from around

the lid. Replenish the ice cubes as needed, but do not let the liquid water overflow. Allow the water to boil for several minutes, but be sure that steam continues coming out because you do not want to boil the pot dry. Using pot holders, remove the pot and contents to an unused burner or other site to cool off. When the pot is cool, remove the lid and dump the melted ice into the sink. Lift out the pudding dish. What is in it? Is it colored? Is the water left in the pot colored? Empty the water in the pot into the sink. The water in the cup is distilled water.

Is your distilled water colorless? Was the colored impurity left behind in the pot? How can you find out if your distilled water is pure? (See Experiment 1.1.)

Science Project Idea

- How does the purified water from Experiment 2.7 compare to hard water? Allow the purified water to evaporate to dryness. No solids should be found in the container. You can compare it to evaporated samples of equal size of hard water, seawater, and pondwater. Hard water can be simulated by dissolving a little Epsom salt in water. How does the distilled water compare in purity to deionized water? To water filtered through purifying cartridges?

Chapter 3

Surface Tension, Adhesion, and Cohesion of Liquid Water

W hy does water descend in a stream when poured from a teapot instead of coming down like rain? Why are soap bubbles round? Why does water move up a strip of paper towel when you dip just one edge in?

The answer to all of these questions is surface tension. Surface tension affects the behavior of all water in the liquid state, whether it is a cupful or an ocean, whether it is trickling or crashing. Blood, sweat, tears—they all exhibit surface tension.

Experiment 3.1

How Many Drops of Water Can a Penny Hold on Its Surface?

Materials

- ✓ tap water
- ✓ penny
- ✓ soap or detergent
- ✓ paper towel
- ✓ flat, waterproof surface
- ✓ eyedropper

Wash a penny well with soap or detergent and water, rinse it very thoroughly with water, and dry it. Place it on a flat, waterproof surface such as a sink counter top. With an eyedropper, add drops of tap water one by one to the surface of the penny. How many drops were you able to add? What shape did the water take? Repeat three times. Find the average number of drops held by the penny.

As the drops are added, they gradually form a dome instead of just flowing off the penny. Each drop raises the surface a little more, stretching the surface as if it were an elastic film until it finally breaks.

The dome shape above the penny is due to a property of liquids called surface tension. Surface tension causes a liquid to act as if it has a thin, elastic film on its surface. The elastic film pulls the surface of the liquid into the smallest possible area.

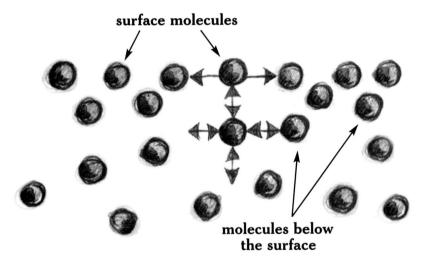

surface molecules

molecules below
the surface

Figure 16.

Unbalanced molecular attraction at the surface of a liquid causes surface tension. Each molecule below the surface attracts and is attracted by molecules on all sides of it. The attractions at the surface pull the surface molecules down and to the sides, but there is nothing above to help balance these attractions. As a result, the surface molecules are pulled together and act like an elastic skin.

Scientists define surface tension as the resistance to an increase in the surface area.

To understand what causes surface tension, consider that liquids are made up of molecules held close to each other because of attractions between the molecules. Each molecule below the surface of the liquid is subject to attractions from all the molecules around it. As a result, the pull on each of the molecules in the interior of the liquid is balanced on all sides of it. Surface molecules, however, have no pull from above. The forces between the surface molecules are not balanced all around them. This results in strengthening the attractive forces between the water molecules at the surface (see Figure 16). It is what causes surface tension. The more polar the molecules are, the stronger the attractive forces between them and the stronger the surface tension. Because water molecules are not only very polar but also have hydrogen bonding between them, water has the highest surface tension of any compound that is liquid at room temperature.

Science Project Ideas

- Compare the surface tension of water to that of other liquids by counting the number of drops on a penny for each, as in Experiment 3.1. Consider liquids in the home such as cooking oil, rubbing alcohol, mineral oil, nail polish remover, and glycerin. Because the size of a drop may vary with the liquid used, measure the volume of the total drops used by placing the same number of drops as used into a graduated cylinder or other measuring device. If there are too few drops to get an accurate reading, double or triple the number of drops in the cylinder, then divide the measurement by two or three for the final volume. Rank the liquids in order of surface tension. How well does your ranking compare with known values? The values may be found in chemistry handbooks in the library or by an Internet search.

- If purified water is used instead of tap water for Experiment 3.1, is there a difference in the number of drops that will form the dome? What if sugar solution is used? What if saltwater is used? Suggest explanations for your results.

- What happens if a nickel or a dime is used instead of a penny? What if a plastic disk about the size of a penny is used? Does the type of plastic make a difference? Obtain data. How do you explain the results?

- What difference do you think the temperature of the water would make in the number of drops on a penny? Why? Test your hypothesis with cold water and then with hot water.

Experiment 3.2

Feeling the Force of Surface Tension

Materials

✓ scissors

✓ sheet of paper

✓ cup of water

✓ isopropyl alcohol, at least 90% (available at supermarkets and drugstores)

You can feel the force of surface tension for yourself. Cut a square of paper into a spiral that has a little handle at the end, as shown in Figure 17. Make the handle about 5 cm (2 in) wide. Pull the spiral down with your fingers and then release it. Holding the handle, make the bottom tip of the spiral touch the surface of some water in a cup. Then pull the spiral upward by the handle.

You will have to jerk the handle upward to get the spiral away from the force of the water's surface tension. The spiral will bounce upward like a spring when you finally get it loose.

Repeat this procedure with rubbing alcohol that is 90 percent or higher concentration instead of water. Which seems to produce a stronger pull, water or alcohol? Which do you think has stronger attractions between its molecules?

Figure 17.

You can feel the force of surface tension for yourself.
a) Cut a spiral out of paper.
b) Lower the end of the spiral to touch the water.

Science Project Ideas

Try the paper spiral experiment on other liquids such as mineral oil, different cooking oils, and glycerin. Is there a difference in the force needed to pull a paper spiral free from each of the liquids? What do the results tell you about the comparative strength of the forces between the molecules in the liquid?

Float a clean needle on water. Photograph or draw the water around the needle. How many needles can float if they are placed close enough to touch? Photograph that, too. Try the same with paper clips.

Experiment 3.3

Cohesive Versus Adhesive Forces

Materials

✓ wax paper
✓ purified water
✓ eyedropper

✓ glass, wood, aluminum, and plastic materials

Place a square of wax paper on a flat, horizontal surface. With an eyedropper, allow one drop of purified water to fall onto the wax paper. What is the shape of the drop?

You can expect to find that the drop forms a slightly flattened sphere resting on a small base. Surface tension acts to pull the water into a sphere, since that is the shape with the smallest surface area possible. The pull of gravity flattens it a bit. This is different from the dome of water that formed on the penny in Experiment 3.1. The water was rounded on the penny, but its base spread out to cover the entire surface on which it rested. What caused the difference in shape? Since water was used for each, it must have been the material on which the water rested that made the difference. Evidently, the metallic penny exerted a large attractive force on the water to get it to spread out. The almost spherical drop of water on the wax paper indicates that the wax paper exerts a much smaller attractive force than the penny.

The attraction of a liquid to a solid surface is called adhesion. The attraction of the molecules of a liquid for each other is called cohesion. Cohesion and adhesion compete with each other when a liquid is in contact with a solid.

Observe the adhesive forces between water and solids such as glass, wood, aluminum, plastic wrap, and other materials by comparing the shape of a drop of purified water on each of the solids. Copy Table 3 into your science notebook to use for writing your observations and conclusions. Add enough rows to the table to document all the different solids chosen for the experiment. Since the cohesive force of water is the same in each case, it will be the adhesive force of the surface materials that makes any difference in the shape of the drop. Prepare a list in which the solids are ranked in order of strength of the adhesive force.

Table 3.

SHAPE OF DROP OF WATER ON SURFACE OF DIFFERENT SOLIDS

Name of Solid	Shape of Drop	Estimate of Comparative Adhesive Strength

Experiment 3.4

Shape of Liquid-Solid Interface

Materials

- ✓ narrow, clear, straight-sided glass container such as a bud vase or test tube
- ✓ clear, straight-sided drinking glass
- ✓ water
- ✓ round wax candle
- ✓ ice

Add some water to a narrow glass container. Hold the container at eye level and observe where the surface of the water meets the glass. What is the shape of the water where it meets the glass?

Next, insert a round wax candle into a clear drinking glass of water. Look at the water around the candle. What do you see?

Did you see that the water curved upward where it touched the inside wall of the glass? Did it curve downward where it met the candle? Figure 18 shows these effects. They are the results of differences between cohesive and adhesive forces.

The adhesive force between the glass and the water is a little stronger than the cohesive force within water. Hence, the adhesive force of the glass pulls the water toward it. With the candle, the adhesive force exerted by the candle is weaker than the cohesive force within water. The water pulls away from the candle.

What happens to the adhesive force at the glass-water interface when hot water is used instead of water at room temperature? Is there a difference? Based on your observations, how do you think the force will change in ice water? Experiment to find out.

Glass is made up of mostly silicon and oxygen atoms. The partially negative oxygen atoms attract the polar water molecules. This creates a strong adhesive force. Candle wax, which is made entirely of carbon and hydrogen atoms, is not at all polar. It has almost no attraction for the polar water molecules.

When you pick up a crumb from the floor with a damp finger, you are taking advantage of the adhesive forces that exist between water and many other substances. In fact, adhesive

Figure 18.
The adhesive forces of different solids can be stronger or weaker than the cohesive force of water.

forces are present all around us, not just between water and other substances. They make it possible for paint to stick to walls, for example, and for ink to stick to paper.

Science Project Idea

◉ Some rough measures of surface tension have already been examined here. Devise a more accurate method for comparing surface tensions by measuring the force required to lift a small, square piece of a solid off the surface of a liquid. You can do this by removing the pan from one side of a hanging beam balance and replacing it with the square held by string. Then, measure the weight on the other side needed to pull the square off the surface of the liquid. A long ruler on a central pivot can be adapted for use as a balance. This measurement of surface tension can be used to compare data when

  a) different solutes are dissolved in water
     (use a glass square).

  b) other solvents are used.

  c) the temperature of the liquid changes.

  d) squares of other materials are substituted for glass.

Experiment 3.5

Raindrops

Materials

✓ water

✓ eyedropper

✓ wax paper

✓ spoon

✓ other liquids, such as cooking oil, mineral oil, and isopropyl alcohol

Drops of water can show in several ways how surface tension affects their behaviors. Use an eyedropper to scatter 8 drops of water onto a flat piece of wax paper. Raise the four corners of the paper to make the drops flow toward each other and observe what happens. With a teaspoon, try to press the drop flat. Can you separate the water back into individual drops?

Surface tension pulls the drops of water into one large drop when they meet. One large drop has a smaller surface area than when broken into several drops. The drop cannot be pressed flat because the surface tension acts to oppose the pressure. A drop of water may spread out when pressed but bounds back when released. If you slap the drop with the spoon, the force of the slap can interrupt the surface tension enough to break the drop into smaller drops.

When an eyedropper is used to deliver a drop of water, the drop elongates a bit before it falls off. This is because the water remaining in the tip is exerting a cohesive force on the drop that holds it back. This is in addition to the adhesive force of the glass on the water. As a result, the drop of water increases in volume as it starts to fall out of the dropper. Use the same dropper as before to find the volume of a fixed number of drops of different liquids, such as cooking oil, mineral oil, and isopropyl alcohol. What conclusions can you draw about the cohesive forces of the different liquids from these observations?

The atmosphere has some unexpected effects on the shape of raindrops. A falling raindrop would be entirely round, thanks to surface tension, were it not for the impact of the air through which it is falling. The air bats away at the bottom of the drop. As a result, the drop is round as it starts the fall, then becomes slightly flattened at the bottom, then indented at the bottom, and finally almost a tube of liquid (see Figure 19). The liquid tube then breaks up into spherical droplets.

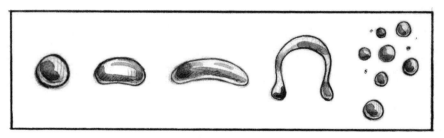

Figure 19.

A raindrop changes shape as it falls due to the upward pressure of the air upon it. The approximate shapes of a cross section are shown in successive stages from left to right. It finally breaks up into spherical raindrops, which go through their own shape changes.

Science Project Ideas

○ Look up scientific reports on the shape of a raindrop. Ask weather forecasters on television programs why they portray the shape when they draw it as tear-shaped. Ask them whether they would consider changing their graphics to reflect reality. You may wish to develop this as a class project. Report on the outcome of your efforts.

○ Super Soakers are super water guns. They can be pumped repeatedly to send out powerful jets of water as far as 15 m (50 ft). Study the water that comes out. Why does the water come out as a jet instead of a series of droplets? Does surface tension play a role? To investigate, try to change the surface tension of the water used. For example, what happens if soapy water is used? What happens if an Epsom-salt solution is used? Be careful to clean up the area with plain water after shooting out solutions. Use the solutions sparingly. Try variations on the jet, such as pulsing it. What happens to the water and why? Can you generate a fountain? Discuss the role of surface tension in all these cases.

Experiment 3.6

How Do Soaps and Detergents Work?

Materials

✓ water

✓ large bowl

✓ talcum powder

✓ toothpick

✓ soap

✓ penny

Fill a large bowl partway with water. Lightly sprinkle a little talcum powder over it. Touch a toothpick to a bar of soap so as to get one end a little soapy. What do you think will happen when you lightly touch the soapy end to the powdered water surface? Try it. Were you correct?

At the point where the toothpick enters the water, the powdered water pulls rapidly away, leaving a wide circle with no powder on it. The surface tension has been weakened where the soap touched the water. The water can no longer support the powder.

What would have happened if you had touched the dome of water on the penny in Experiment 3.1 with the soapy toothpick? Try it.

Soap and detergent molecules are made up of long chains of carbon and hydrogen atoms that have, at one end, a group that is ionic, or polar, and that "likes" water but "dislikes" nonpolar liquids. The remainder of the long molecule is nonpolar. It "dislikes" water but "likes" polar liquids. Fats and grease are nonpolar. They not only make clothes dirty but help other dirt to cling to them. The nonpolar end of a soap or detergent molecule tends to be soluble in grease and oil. As a result, the nonpolar ends dissolve in the dirt particles. The other end of each long soap or detergent molecule (the polar end) sticks out of the dirt into the water, where it is soluble. This causes a piece of dirt or fat to have soap particles within it that are sticking out of it on all sides, as shown in Figure 20. The water-soluble ends that are sticking out carry the dirt off clothing or carry grease off a dish to mix with the water.

Soaps and detergents also help water soak into fabrics. The polar head of a soap molecule disrupts the surface tension of the water so that it wets the fabric.

Science Project Ideas

○ Test the effectiveness of different soaps and detergents on a few drops of oil in water to visually compare how well each can make the oil mix into the water. Rank the soaps and/or detergents accordingly in your report.

○ Use garden soil to dirty samples of cotton fabric. Each sample should be the same size and have a square of dirt

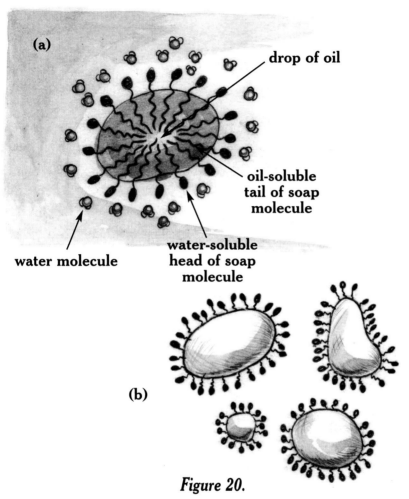

(a)

drop of oil

oil-soluble
tail of soap
molecule

water-soluble
head of soap
molecule

water molecule

(b)

Figure 20.

a) Soap and detergent molecules have one end that is soluble
    in water but not soluble in oil. The rest of the molecule is
    soluble in oil but not in water. The oil-soluble ends of
    the molecules embed themselves in a drop of oil, as shown.
    The water-soluble ends stick out into the water all around
    the outside of the drop. The drop of oil moves into the
    water to be rinsed away.

b) Grease particles on a dish are coated by soap. Water will
    carry the soapy particles off the dish.

on it of the same size. Be careful to spread out the same amount of dirt on each sample. Investigate how well brand-name soaps and detergents clean the dirt off the samples. Use visual observations of the dirt remaining on the sample after washing to compare the effectiveness of the soaps and detergents.

a) Test the soaps and detergents using warm water at the same temperature for each.

b) Repeat using hot water.

c) Find out which soaps and detergents work in cold water.

Which brand-name is the best?

Do brand-name soaps and detergents work equally well with different fabrics? Test one of the brand-name soaps or detergents with other fabrics such as wool, rayon, silk, nylon, acrylic, and others. Then test other brand-name cleaners. Water temperature may yield some differences, so be sure to test each of your soaps and detergents over the same range of temperatures.

Experiment 3.7

What Is a Soap Bubble?

Materials

- ✓ tap water
- ✓ liquid dish detergent
- ✓ glycerin
- ✓ drinking straw
- ✓ bowl

- ✓ measuring cup, or graduated cylinder
- ✓ soap bubble pipe or ring
- ✓ freezer

Bubbles are beautiful as they lightly float through the air with an ever-changing display of colors. They are also fascinating scientific objects, illustrating both physics principles and unique chemical structures. There are many recipes for making bubbles, all using different proportions of water, liquid detergent, and glycerin. All the recipes work. Some people are allergic to glycerin, so if you have not handled it before, get tested or test yourself with a dot of it on your skin well before you do this experiment. If you get any redness on the skin or have any other reaction to the glycerin, do not use it.

Use a measuring cup or graduated cylinder to make up a bubble solution of 85 mL tap water, 10 mL liquid dish detergent, and 5 mL glycerin. Obtain a soap bubble pipe or ring, preferably one that blows a single bubble. Blow up a

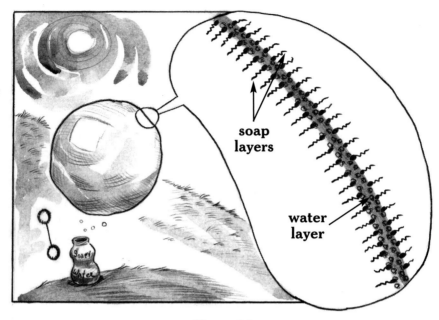

Figure 21.

The skin of a soap bubble has a water layer sandwiched between two soap layers. The outer layers protect the water inside from quick evaporation. Surface tension gives the bubble its globular shape.

bubble and stop blowing so that the bubble rests on the pipe. Watch it. What do you observe?

The bubble will maintain a spherical shape with shining colors, then gradually shrink until it snaps out of existence. The spherical shape is a clue that surface tension is at work. The shape is maintained while the bubble shrinks.

The detergent is not there to increase the surface tension, although this is a common misconception. Instead, it is there to decrease surface tension. The surface tension of plain water is too strong to produce lasting bubbles. Blow through a straw into a bowl of tap water to try to produce bubbles. What happens to any bubbles that form?

Soaps and detergents decrease the surface tension of the water, as was observed in Experiment 3.6. They allow the bubble to form without collapsing due to the force of surface tension.

The surface film that you see on a soap bubble is actually three layers, as shown in Figure 21. The middle layer is water. The water is sandwiched between two layers of soap molecules. The polar heads of the soap molecules push into the water, while the rest of the long molecules extend outward from it, providing the two outside layers of the bubble sandwich. The soap layers help to protect the thin inside layer of water from rapidly evaporating. Evaporation of water is what causes a soap bubble to collapse.

Can a bubble be frozen? Try it and explain what happens.

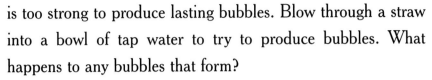

Science Project Ideas

- Experiment with different materials such as string, pipe cleaners, and wires of different metals to make a ring from which to blow bubbles. Is one material superior to others? Why?

Because bubbles contract to the shape with the least surface area, you can find the shape of the smallest area for films around three-dimensional wire frames without going through the mathematical work. With the help of an adult, solder or glue together narrow copper rods to make up frames in different shapes. Make a cube, a tetrahedron, an octahedron, and other polyhedrons. Try making other shapes as well. Tie a long thread to each one. Hold one frame by its thread, dip it into the bubble solution, and then remove it. Allow it to hang over the solution to drain and observe the film as it shrinks to the smallest skin that can envelope the frame. Display the results as drawings or, better yet, photographs. Explain the role of surface tension in the shapes.

Investigate the role of glycerin in the bubble solution. For example, make a starter solution containing 85 mL water and 10 mL liquid dish detergent (no glycerin). Make another solution to which 2 mL glycerin are added. Then make additional solutions with, successively, 5 mL, 10 mL, and 20 mL of glycerin added, for a total of five solutions. Measure how long a bubble made from each solution lasts. Repeat several times for each solution and average the time for it. What do your experiments tell you about the role of glycerin in making bubbles?

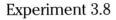

Experiment 3.8

Capillarity: Water Can Walk up the Sides of a Tube

Materials

✓ tap water at room temperature
✓ plain drinking glass
✓ 2 glass or plastic drinking straws, one of which is narrower than the other
✓ pen with waterproof ink
✓ ruler
✓ glass eyedropper
✓ hot tap water
✓ icy tap water

Drinking straws can introduce you to one of the special processes of nature, a process that often goes unobserved. If you can obtain glass straws or narrow glass tubing with fire-polished ends, the effect that is examined in this experiment shows up more. However, it can also be seen with plastic straws.

Start with a glass filled partway with tap water. Allow it to stand for at least 5 minutes to bring it to room temperature. Obtain two straws of different diameters. Mark a line with waterproof ink across the width of each straw 4 cm (1½ in) from one end. Holding one straw vertically with the ink line at its bottom end, lower the straw into the water to the level of the mark. Then cap the straw tightly with your index finger and lift it out of the water. Is any water inside the straw? Hold the straw over the glass and gradually release your finger so that the water drips out. Repeat the process as needed until you can get the water to run out in drops. There will be a little water left in the straw. With a ruler, measure the length of the column of water left in the straw.

Repeat the above with the second straw. Does one straw have a longer column of water left in it than the other one? If so, was it the narrower one or the wider one?

Although most of the water drops out of the two straws, a little remains in each. The water that stays in the straws defies gravity! What holds the water in the straws, and why is there a difference in the length of the water columns?

There are adhesive forces between the straw and the water that attract the water toward the wall of the straw. When the straw is removed from the water and uncapped, the water level drops down until the weight of the water equals the adhesive force attracting it. The column of water in the wider straw weighs more than a column of the same length in the narrower straw. The adhesive force of the wider straw is not great enough to pull the greater mass of water to the same height as in the narrower straw.

The process that causes a liquid to rise in a narrow tube is called capillarity or capillary action. It is due to the adhesive force between the walls of the tube and the liquid. The narrower

Figure 22.

CAPILLARY ACTION

The smaller the diameter of a tube, the higher the water rises in it.

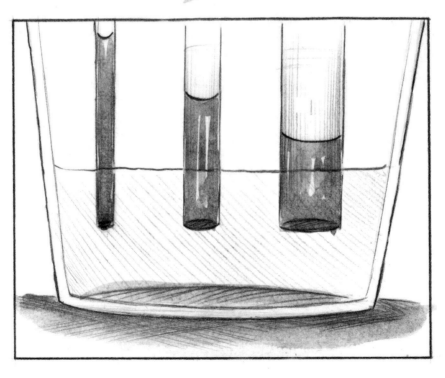

the tube, the higher water rises in it. Water, because of its strong polarity, tends to show high capillarity compared to other liquids. Glass exerts a stronger adhesive force on water than do most plastics. Figure 22 shows capillarity in three tubes of varying diameters. The ends of the tubes have simply been lowered into the water.

Does capillarity depend on temperature? The tip of a glass eyedropper is usually quite narrow and shows enough capillary action in water to be easily visible. (If you can find a long tube as narrow as the neck of the eyedropper, use that instead.) Remove the rubber cap from an eyedropper. Dip the narrow end of the dropper at least 1 cm (½ in) into water at room temperature, hold it there for at least 30 seconds, and then remove it. Record the height of the water in the narrow end. Shake out the water in the eyedropper. Repeat but use hot water this time. Finally, repeat with ice water. Is there a difference in the capillary action depending on the temperature? Which causes the water to rise up in the tube the most, hot water or cold water?

Anywhere that water moves through a crevice, capillary action appears. That is why water creeps up a paper towel and up the roots and stem of a plant and the trunk of a tree. Capillarity helps the blood in your body move through the tiniest blood vessels. The lives of both animals and plants depend on it.

Science Project Ideas

- How does material used to make a tube affect the capillary action of water in a narrow tube? Compare tubes that are of the same diameter but made of different materials.

- Does capillary action take place with a narrow glass tube dipped into an acetone-type nail polish remover? Into a non-acetone polish remover? Into cooking oil? Find out and explain.

- Do you think that capillary action will move water up a glass tube that has been coated inside with a little cooking oil? Try it. Why do you get the observed result?

- Would you like to make two-color celery? Capillarity makes this possible. Start with a wilted stalk. Have an adult make one slice up the length of the stalk almost to where it branches. Put food dye into one glass of water and a different color dye into another glass of water. Stick one end of the split celery into one glass and the other end into the other glass. Take photographs at intervals to show what happens and supply an explanation for each. Can you make a two-colored carnation? Can you make a polka-dot carnation?

Experiment 3.9

Paper Chromatography

Materials

✓ 2 ballpoint pens with black washable ink (preferably 1 Flair black pen and 1 pen of another brand)

✓ paper filter made for coffee maker, or white paper towel

✓ scissors

✓ purified water

✓ 3 plain drinking glasses

✓ pencil

✓ paper clip

✓ ruler

Although capillary action has been known for many centuries, even if not identified as such, chemists did not begin to take advantage of this simple process until the mid-twentieth century. Capillary action can be used to quickly separate the components of gaseous or liquid mixtures. The results make it possible to analyze the mixtures or to physically separate them for research purposes. Paper chromatography is the simplest of the processes that use capillarity. It will be used in this experiment to separate the components of black washable ink.

Obtain a paper filter used for coffee makers or, if not available, white paper towel. Cut a strip about 2.5 cm (1 in) wide and 17.5 cm (7 in) long. About 2.5 cm from one end, use a pencil to draw a line across the width of the strip (see Figure 23). Make a dot about 0.3 cm (⅛ in) across in the middle of the line with a black washable-ink ballpoint pen. Draw another line with a pencil across the width 10 cm (4 in) above the first line. Hang the strip on a pencil by folding the unmarked end over it. Place the pencil across the top of an empty drinking glass and adjust the paper strip so that the end hangs a little less than 1 cm (about ½ in) above the bottom. Secure the paper in that position on the pencil with a paper clip. Remove the pencil assembly and set it aside on a clean surface to allow the black dot to dry.

Pour purified water into the glass to a height of almost 2 cm (¾ in) above the bottom. Hang the pencil on the glass so that the bottom of the paper strip dips into the water.

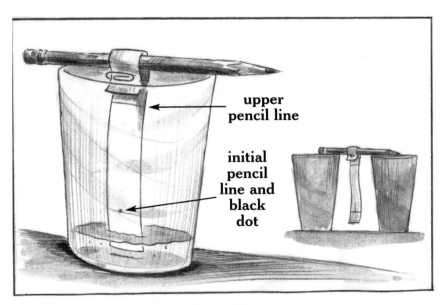

upper pencil line

initial pencil line and black dot

Figure 23.

PAPER CHROMATOGRAPHY

The water will start rising up the paper. As soon as it reaches the pencil line at the upper end of the strip, lift the pencil and attached paper from the glass. Suspend it between two clean, dry glasses to let the paper strip air dry.

When the paper strip is dry, measure the distance that each color traveled from the initial pencil line or, if only black appears, the distance that the black traveled. You can mark these with pencil on your paper strip. You already know the distance that the water traveled. Next, you will calculate the retention factor for each color, including black. The retention factor, R_f, compares the distance that a color travels to the distance that the water travels in the same time. Calculate the retention factor for each color as follows:

$$R_f = \frac{\text{distance the color travels}}{\text{distance the water travels}}$$

Repeat all of the above for the other brand of black washable ballpoint ink.

How many colors appear on each strip? Are the two inks each made only of black or of a combination of colors? Are the two inks the same? If the same colors appear, they may not be made of the same chemical. The R_f may be able to tell you whether or not they are the same.

The distances traveled in the same time by the water and the colors are due to capillarity. As you saw in Experiment 3.8, capillarity starts with adhesion. Paper is made of tiny fibers that draw water up into them. The adhesive force of the paper is a little stronger than the combination of the opposing cohesive force of water and the downward pull of gravity. As a result, the water rises up the paper. The water carries the color molecules up with it, although it is unable to raise them as high.

Colored chemicals are not the only ones that can be separated by paper chromatography. An ultraviolet lamp can make some chemicals on the paper strip visible by causing them to glow. In other cases, a light spray of a substance can react with one of the test substances to form a colored product.

Science Project Ideas

Be sure to include the labeled paper strip (chromatogram) with your science project display.

- Use paper chromatography to test different washable colored inks to see their components. Based on retention factors, find out whether any use the same chemical for a particular ink color.

- Are the colors in the food coloring kit sold in the supermarket each a single color or combinations of colors?

If you can find a second kit by a different manufacturer, find out if the same dyes are used to make up the food colors as in the other kit. Explain why combinations are sometimes used rather than a single dye color.

Use paper chromatography to determine the separate colors that make up the color of the coating on an M&M candy. To concentrate the color, wet the candy, dab it on the strip, let the strip dry, and repeat the dabbing over and over until the color is strong. Also, try paper chromatography on unsweetened orange or purple Kool-Aid. Use only enough water for an entire package to make a paste and apply a dot of it with a toothpick. Look for other supermarket products to test using this method.

How does the paper used affect the retention factor and the results in Experiment 3.9? Try coarser and finer papers, and try different types of paper. Can fabrics be used for chromatography? Which ones? Why?

Surface tension forces are involved in the processes that make life possible for all living creatures, that allow the formation of waves in the oceans, that are needed to form clouds in the skies, that enable rain to fall in drops, that slow evaporation from the oceans and other bodies of water, and that moderate the climate. Water is unique in that it has the highest surface tension of all liquid compounds that exist at normal temperatures.

Chapter 4

Chemical Properties of Water

Thousands have lived without love, not one without water.

— W. H. Auden, *poet*

The physical properties of water are those that result from water's makeup, such as its ability to dissolve other substances, its freezing point, and surface tension. In physical experiments, the water's makeup, and therefore its identity, remains the same throughout the activity. It is water at the beginning and still water at the end. The changes that water goes through during the hydrological cycle—from the ground to the atmosphere to rain or snow and back to the ground again—are all physical changes. These physical changes do not change the makeup of the water.

On the other hand, a chemical change occurs when the water molecule is broken apart to form one or more molecules with a different identity. In a chemical reaction, bonds between atoms are broken, and new combinations of the atoms make new products. The water that was present at the beginning of the chemical reaction is gone. The atoms that were present at the beginning of the reaction are still there at the end, but they are bonded differently.

Water is a very stable chemical. It takes considerable energy to disrupt the bonds between its hydrogen and oxygen atoms. As an example of its stability, consider that water is used to put out fires, not to start them. It puts out fires mainly by simply blanketing the flames, preventing atmospheric oxygen from getting to the fire's fuel. Also, as the fire heats the water and changes it to a gas (which is a physical change), the water takes heat from the flames. As a result, the vaporization helps to cool the fire.

What are some of the chemical properties of water? That is, how does water react chemically to form different products? A chemical property that has already been examined is that water can be broken up by electrolysis to form hydrogen gas and oxygen gas (see Experiment 1.1). Some other chemical properties of water will be examined in this chapter.

Experiment 4.1

Water Reacts With Metal Oxides

Materials

✓ safety goggles

✓ stainless steel teaspoon

✓ lime

✓ ceramic cup

✓ purified water

✓ medicine dropper

✓ glass jar with lid

✓ vinegar

At room temperatures, water reacts violently with very active metals such as sodium and potassium. As a result, you will never find these metals in the home or anywhere else unless specially protected because water is always in the air. Moderately active metals like aluminum and magnesium react with hot steam. If you are wondering why some cooking pots are made of aluminum even though it reacts with hot steam, it is because aluminum exposed to air becomes coated with a very tight, protective layer of aluminum oxide.

Water does react with ordinary lime, the white powder sold in garden supply or building supply stores. Lime is calcium oxide, CaO, a compound of calcium (Ca) and oxygen (O). Compounds of metals and oxygen are called metal oxides, so lime is a metal oxide. Since you only need a bit of lime for this experiment, perhaps a neighbor who gardens or a local builder can give you some.

Put on safety goggles. Place about a teaspoonful of lime into a ceramic cup. With a medicine dropper, add three drops of water to the lime. What happens? Feel the outside bottom of the cup. Keep adding water drop by drop until the dropper is empty. Then, while stirring with the spoon, add enough water to make up half a cupful.

The lime bubbles as water is added. It is reacting with water. The reaction produces heat. The heat vaporizes some of the water with a sizzling effect. Once the lime has completely reacted, additional water helps to cool the cup. The reaction that takes place when water is added is shown below in words, followed by the same reaction in chemical shorthand.

calcium oxide   and   water   react to yield   calcium hydroxide

$$CaO + H_2O \rightarrow Ca(OH)_2$$

The solution of calcium hydroxide that you have made is called limewater. Calcium hydroxide is only slightly soluble in water, so some of it may settle to the bottom of the cup. Pour the limewater into a glass jar and cap it tightly. Store it in a safe place to use in Experiment 4.6. Do not handle the limewater with bare fingers. If you wish to discard the limewater, add vinegar drop-wise to the cup while stirring until all of the calcium hydroxide is reacted and disappears. You may then flush it down the drain with water. If any lime is left in the cup, treat it with vinegar again. The spoon can be cleaned by rinsing it with cold water.

Any remaining lime may be stored in a sealed plastic bag in a dry area.

Science Project Idea

- For centuries, brick walls have been constructed by layering brick in rows upon each other with a thick paste of mortar in between. The mortar hardens to a firm layer that binds the bricks into a permanent structure. To make mortar, water is slowly added to lime in the proportion of 20 g lime to 10 mL water. After mixing, 20 g sand are added. Then more water is slowly added until the mixture has the consistency of paste. Does mortar harden under water? What is known about the chemistry of mortar? What is the purpose of the lime? Of the sand? Of the water? Make up samples using different proportions of lime, water, and sand to see how the product varies with composition. Do not handle the lime unless you are wearing gloves.

Experiment 4.2

Does Iron React With Water?

Materials

✓ steel wool pad, soap-free   ✓ water

✓ scissors   ✓ 2 cups

✓ glass jar with tight lid   ✓ 2 pieces of paper

We have all seen that iron rusts when exposed to water. Does this mean that iron reacts with water? To find out, obtain a clean piece of soap-free steel wool. Steel wool is made mostly of iron. Pull the pad apart a little and cut it in three pieces with scissors. Place one piece of steel wool in a glass jar, add water until it is completely covered, and tightly cap the jar. Place a second piece into a dry cup. Wet the third piece and place that one into another dry cup.

Cover each of the two cups lightly with a piece of paper. Put the two cups and the jar in a place where they will remain untouched and out of the sun. Inspect them for change every few days for 2 to 3 weeks. Copy Table 4 into your science notebook and write your observations in it.

How can your observations be explained?

When iron reacts with oxygen to form rust, water acts as a catalyst to speed up the reaction. Without a catalyst, the reaction

Table 4.

DOES IRON REACT WITH WATER?

Steel wool treatment	Observation				
	Day 4	Day 7	Day 10	Day 13	Day 16
Covered by water					
Dry, in air					
Wet, in air					

of iron and oxygen takes place very slowly. Water speeds up the reaction but does not itself undergo any chemical change.

Continue Experiment 4.2 for a period of several months. What happens? Do the outcomes agree with the conclusions you have already reached?

Science Project Ideas

○ How does an increase in temperature affect the rusting of wet steel wool in the air? What are the implications of your results for the use of steel for outdoor purposes?

○ Underwater wrecks of iron ships have been found in excellent condition despite years at the site. Why do they last so long? Carry out experiments to see if the low temperature is the reason.

Experiment 4.3

Water Makes Some Reactions Possible

Materials

✓ baking soda

✓ cream of tartar

✓ small, plain drinking glass

✓ teaspoon

✓ water

✓ baking powder

✓ paper or cloth towel

Place half a teaspoon of baking soda ($NaHCO_3$) into a small, plain glass. Add half a teaspoon of cream of tartar

($KHC_4H_4O_6$). You can find cream of tartar in the baking section of a supermarket. Mix the baking soda and cream of tartar thoroughly. What happens?

Add half a teaspoon of water. What happens now? Why did the water make such a difference? Add water to the glass until it is about one-fourth filled. Stir well. What do you see now? How do you explain it? Rinse out the glass with water and dry it with a cloth or paper towel.

Upon adding the water, did the powders begin bubbling? What color was the water after the bubbling stopped? When the additional water was stirred, did the solution become clear?

The reaction between cream of tartar and baking soda produces carbon dioxide as one of the products. The carbon dioxide is what you saw bubbling out. The other products are very soluble in water, but half a teaspoon of water is too small to dissolve all of these products. Further addition of water dissolves the remainder.

Why does the reaction between baking soda and cream of tartar not take place until water is added? The water is needed to dissolve the two solids. The baking soda and cream of tartar are made up of ions. In water, each ion becomes surrounded by envelopes of water molecules, as discussed in Chapter 1. Then they are able to move around separately from each other. In a liquid, the particles are moving around all the time. As a result, ions from the baking soda come into contact with ions from the cream of tartar and react.

The baking powder used in baking breads and cakes is made up of cream of tartar, baking soda, and cornstarch. Baking powder keeps well for long periods as long as no water gets into the container. The cornstarch is added to absorb any water from the air that gets in. When placed into a cake or bread recipe, the baking powder gradually comes in contact with the water mixed in with the flour and other ingredients. The same reaction as in this experiment takes place: carbon dioxide is released. The carbon dioxide causes the cake or bread to rise.

Predict what will happen when you add a few drops of water to some dry baking powder. Try it. Was your prediction correct?

Science Project Ideas

○ Obtain a recipe for bread or cake that uses baking powder. What happens to your bread or cake if it is made with extra cream of tartar? With extra baking soda? **Under adult supervision**, bake samples for display, evaluate them, and discuss the results.

How does raising the temperature affect the reaction in this experiment? How does lowering the temperature affect it? Based only on these limited results, how does temperature affect a reaction? Illustrate your observations with drawings or photographs.

How does increasing the baking temperature affect a cake or bread made using baking powder? **Under adult supervision**, bake samples to show the results.

Experiment 4.4

Acids, Bases, and Indicators

Materials

✓ red cabbage

✓ measuring cup

✓ small pot with lid

✓ purified water

✓ **an adult**

✓ stove burner with vent fan

✓ jar with lid

✓ white vinegar

✓ clear drinking glass

✓ clean, dry medicine dropper

✓ sink

✓ stainless steel or plastic tablespoon

✓ clear, soap-free ammonia (can be purchased at the supermarket)

Acids and bases are two chemical groups that are of major importance in chemistry. The acids and bases that will be studied here are those that are present in water.

Acids have a sour taste. The tart flavor of lemon juice, tomatoes, sour apples, sauerkraut, pickles, and vinegar is caused by acids. Soft drinks and wine also contain acids. Acids are found in the digestive fluids in our stomachs and in the amino acids that form proteins. Vitamin C and aspirin are acids. A powerful acid called sulfuric acid is the biggest selling synthetic chemical in the nation. Bases, on the other hand, taste bitter and feel slippery. Ammonia, harsh soaps, and baking soda are all bases. Some acids and bases burn the tongue, so it is not wise to taste them unless they are known to be safe.

A property that all acids and bases share is that they cause color changes in certain materials called indicators. In this activity, you will make an indicator and use it to identify acids and bases.

Start with a head of red cabbage. The chemical that causes the red color is what you wish to extract from the cabbage. Tear some leaves into enough small pieces to fill a cup. Place the leaves into a small pot, as shown in Figure 24, and add purified water until they are covered. **Under adult supervision**, heat the water to boiling and boil it for five minutes. Cover the pot and allow it to cool to room temperature. Pour off the red liquid into a jar and screw on the lid. Discard the wet cabbage leaves into a garbage container. The red cabbage indicator will keep for about a week in the refrigerator and can be frozen indefinitely.

Figure 24.

MAKING A RED
CABBAGE INDICATOR

Acids in water turn red cabbage extract to a red to purple color, whereas bases turn it blue to green. Thus, red cabbage extract is an indicator that can be used to distinguish between an acid and a base.

Pour about ¼ cup of white vinegar into a plain, colorless drinking glass. Use a clean, dry medicine dropper to add 5 drops of red cabbage extract to the vinegar. Swirl the cup of liquid. What color appears? Is vinegar acidic or basic? Discard the contents into the sink with running water.

Repeat the above test with a tablespoon of soap-free clear ammonia. Work rapidly because ammonia is irritating. If you have a stove vent fan, carry this out under the fan, or do this outdoors. What color appeared? Is ammonia acidic or basic? After you have carried out the test, immediately discard the solution into the sink and rinse with running water.

Chemically, it has been found that what makes a substance act as an acid in water is that it splits apart to release the hydrogen ion H^+. The strongly polar water acts to pull the hydrogen ion away from the rest of the molecule. Vinegar is a dilute water solution of a solid called acetic acid. The following equation shows what happens when acetic acid is dissolved in the water.

$$HC_2H_3O_2 \quad \rightarrow \quad H^+ \quad + \quad C_2H_3O_2^-$$

acetic acid   yields   hydrogen ion   and   acetate ion

To show that the ions are surrounded by water molecules, they are often written as H^+ (*aq*) and $C_2H_3O_2^-$ (*aq*), where (*aq*) stands for *aqueous* (which means "water"). The equation can be written as

$$HC_2H_3O_2 \text{ (aq)} \rightarrow H^+ \text{ (aq)} + C_2H_3O_2^- \text{ (aq)}$$

It is the H^+ (*aq*) that changes the color of an indicator. The $C_2H_3O_2^-$ (*aq*) does not affect an indicator.

All bases in water release the hydroxide ion OH^- into the solution. Some bases such as sodium hydroxide (NaOH), a solid that is commonly called lye, simply split into ions when in water.

$$NaOH \text{ (s)} \rightarrow Na+ \text{ (aq)} + OH^- \text{ (aq)}$$

In such equations, (*s*) stands for a solid.

Some bases, such as ammonia, react with water to form the hydroxide ion. Ammonia, NH_3, is a gas. The ammonia sold in supermarkets is a solution of ammonia molecules in water. When added to water, some of the ammonia reacts with it to give ammonium ions and hydroxide ions as follows.

$$NH_3 \text{ (aq)} + H_2O \text{ (l)} \rightarrow NH_4^+ \text{ (aq)} + OH^- \text{ (aq)}$$

ammonia and water   yield ammonium ion and hydroxide ion

It is the OH^- (*aq*) that changes the color of indicator papers to show that a base is present. Neither Na^+ (*aq*) nor NH_4^+ (*aq*) affect an indicator.

Science Project Ideas

- Test water solutions of materials in the home with red cabbage indicator. Which materials in the home are acids? Which are bases? Which are neither (neutral)? Construct a table of your results.

- Red cabbage is not the only vegetable that changes color in the presence of acids and/or bases. Numerous other vegetable and flower colors respond to acids and to bases. Turmeric and marigold petals are examples, as are beet and cherry juices. How many colored fruits and vegetables can you find whose extracts change colors with vinegar or ammonia? To display the results, you can use strips of white absorbent paper that have been soaked in an indicator and allowed to dry. When an indicator strip is touched with a bit of acid, it changes color. A touch of base shows a different color.

Experiment 4.5

Do Acids and Bases Neutralize Each Other?

Materials

✓ safety goggles

✓ stainless steel or plastic teaspoon

✓ limewater (from Experiment 4.1)

✓ lemon juice

✓ purified water

✓ 2 white cups

✓ 2 medicine droppers

✓ red cabbage indicator (see Experiment 4.4)

What happens when an acid is added to a base? Does it affect the base at all and, if so, how? Red cabbage indicator can help find some answers. In this experiment, you will start with a strongly basic solution (many hydroxide ions) with cabbage indicator in it. Then, acid will be added little by little to the basic solution. The acid will be supplied by lemon juice.

Copy Table 5 into your science notebook and use it to keep a record of your observations. Put on your safety goggles. Place 5 mL (1 teaspoon) of limewater from Experiment 4.1 into a white cup. Add 4 drops of red cabbage indicator. Gently swirl the liquid a few times to mix it all up. In your notebook (Table 5), note the color of the solution in the cup. Do you think that this solution is acidic or basic (refer to the colors in Experiment

4.4)? Next, add lemon juice to the cup drop by drop while you gently swirl the solution. Keep count of the drops added and record the colors as you see changes. Add additional columns to Table 5 if needed. Keep adding the lemon juice until a color is reached that doesn't change on further addition of juice.

Table 5.
RANGE OF COLORS FOR RED CABBAGE INDICATOR

Number of drops of lemon juice added to limewater	0						
Color							red

Next, add 1 teaspoon of purified water to a clean white cup. Add 4 drops of red cabbage indicator to it and swirl it. What color is the water now? Record your observation in your notebook to show the color of water with cabbage indicator. Purified water is neither acidic nor basic; it is neutral. The color of the purified water with indicator is the color of a neutral solution. Now, you have all the information needed to understand why the indicator changes color as you add more and more of the acidic lemon juice. What is your explanation?

At the start, the solution was green due to the hydroxide ions from the limewater. As the acidic lemon juice was added, the color gradually changed. How did it change? Was the final color red? If so, it was due to the presence of hydrogen ions. Red indicates an acid solution.

What was the color of the purified water? Do you think it is a neutral solution?

The hydrogen ions (H^+) being added reacted with the hydroxide ions (OH^-) already there. Together, they formed water as shown in the following equation.

$$H^+ \, (aq) \quad + \quad OH^- \, (aq) \quad \rightarrow \quad H_2O \, (l)$$

hydrogen ion   plus   hydroxide ion   yield   water

As the added hydrogen ions removed hydroxide ions, the solution became less and less basic. The indicator showed this by changing color. Eventually, practically all of the hydroxide ions were neutralized by the hydrogen ions. The solution was neutral, the same way that water itself is. Now, as more acid continued to be added, the solution simply became more and more strongly acid.

What do you think will happen if you start with a lemon juice solution containing red cabbage indicator and gradually add drops of limewater to it? Try it. Explain the results.

Science Project Ideas

○ You can write secret messages on white paper with red cabbage indicator solution and allow it to dry. When sprayed lightly with lemon juice, the message will appear. Various other indicators can be used for such hidden messages. Report on how to make and use other indicator "secret messages."

○ Nonmetal oxides such as carbon dioxide, sulfur dioxide, and sulfur trioxide react with water to form acids. They are major air pollutants. Why has their presence in the air become important recently? What does water have to do with it?

○ Acid pollution has defaced or destroyed marble monuments around the world. Test samples of marble to find out how acid affects them. Is any one type of marble affected more than others? Or less? What is the reaction that takes place? How can the marble be protected? What is being done to restore damaged marble monuments?

Experiment 4.6

How Powerful Are the Hydrogen Ions?

Materials

- ✓ red cabbage indicator (see Experiment 4.4)
- ✓ several white china cups
- ✓ clean, dry stainless steel or plastic teaspoons
- ✓ purified water
- ✓ clean, dry medicine dropper
- ✓ milk
- ✓ apple juice
- ✓ Sprite, regular
- ✓ Sprite, sugar-free
- ✓ milk of magnesia
- ✓ borax
- ✓ baking soda
- ✓ salt
- ✓ sugar
- ✓ aspirin
- ✓ antacid tablet
- ✓ universal indicator paper

The term *pH* is probably seen most often in newspapers with respect to acid rain and acid lakes. The *p* stands for "potenz" or "power," and the *H* for hydrogen. It describes the degree to which a substance acts as an acid. A pH of 7 is neutral; below 7 is acidic and above 7 is basic as diagramed in Figure 25. Acidity, basicity, and pH are tied together. The lower the pH, the more acidic the water solution is and the less basic. The higher the pH, the less acidic it is and the more basic. Each time the pH goes up by one unit, say from 8 to 9, the water solution is

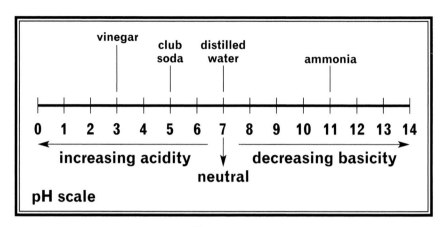

Figure 25.

On this pH scale, the strongest acid has a pH value of 0, while the strongest base has a pH value of 14. Anything with a pH value of 7 is considered neutral.

one-tenth as acidic as before and ten times as basic. Conversely, when the pH goes down from, say, 5 to 4, the water solution has become ten times as acidic and one-tenth as basic as before.

Purified water should have a pH of 7. Water is considered fit to drink if it has a pH between 6.5 and 8.5. Above that range, it is too basic and below, too acidic.

Red cabbage indicator provides only a rough measure of pH but it is quite adequate for many purposes. Table 6 gives the approximate pH values for the red cabbage colors in the order that they appear going from acid to very basic. The colors that you perceive may differ slightly depending on your eyesight. What is the pH for a strongly basic solution? What is the pH range for acidic solutions?

Table 6.
APPROXIMATE pH FOR THE RANGE OF COLORS
OF RED CABBAGE INDICATOR

Color	red	purple	purple-blue	blue	blue-green	greenish
Approximate pH	2	4	6	8	10	12

You can now use red cabbage indicator to find the approximate pH of a variety of household materials. Copy Table 7 into your science notebook and use it to keep a record of your observations. You already know the red cabbage indicator colors for ammonia solution, vinegar, limewater, lemon juice, and purified water, so fill those in first. You will be testing the following liquids: milk, apple juice, both regular and sugar-free Sprite, and milk of magnesia. For each of the liquids, find the pH by placing a teaspoon of the liquid into a clean white cup and adding 4 drops of red cabbage indicator to it. Swirl the solution and observe the color. Also, test the following solids: borax, baking soda, salt, sugar, aspirin, and an antacid tablet. The solids need to be dissolved in water before testing. Place about half a teaspoon of solid into a clean cup and add several teaspoons of purified water. Swirl for about 30 seconds. Pour off the clear solution into another cup and add 4 drops of red cabbage indicator to the solution. Swirl, and note the color. Rinse the cups with purified water until clean. Repeat for each of the solids.

Table 7.

pH OF SOME HOUSEHOLD MATERIALS

Test material	Color	pH	Test material	Color	pH
ammonia			apple juice		
vinegar			milk of magnesia		
limewater			borax		
lemon juice			baking soda		
purified water			salt		
Sprite			sugar		
Sprite, sugar-free			aspirin		
milk			antacid		

Although red cabbage juice is a good homemade indicator, you can instead use a drop of your test solution on dry universal indicator paper to find the pH. Universal indicator paper can be purchased at some garden stores and hardware stores. You may be able to obtain some from your school science teacher. The universal indicator paper strips are made of a mixture of indicators so that they have a wide range of different color changes to indicate the presence of acids and bases of different pH, wider than that of red cabbage extract. A printed sample of colors for each pH is provided with the strips. Individuals who are totally color blind may need to obtain a pH meter to be able to carry out pH experiments.

Now you are able to carry out projects and investigations that require a measurement of pH.

Science Project Ideas

○ Does the method of preparation affect the colors of red cabbage extract in response to different pHs? Try making the extract by soaking the leaves in cold water or by boiling them, by soaking for different lengths of time, and by cutting the leaves into small pieces or by using a blender to mash the leaves to a fine slurry. Compare the colors obtained at different pHs. What differences do you find and how do you explain them?

The pigment that gives red cabbage its color is called flavin and is also found in plums, grapes, and apple skins. Make indicators from one or more of these fruits and determine how they react to pH. Do you think that the molecule that makes the color is the same for each? Explain.

You can make permanent displays of color changes due to pH by using strips of paper soaked in the extract and allowed to dry. A drop of liquid placed on a clean dry portion of the indicator paper will show a color change depending on the pH. Coffee filters work well when cut into strips for this purpose. After you have set up your display of labeled papers, protect them from the air by placing them in colorless, transparent report folders sealed around the edges with tape.

By combining several indicators, it may be possible to get a mixed indicator with a more striking range of color changes over a wider pH range. Prepare indicators from different home and plant sources as suggested previously and try different combinations. Describe and chart both your successes and failures. If you find a particularly good combination, discuss possible publication of your results with a science teacher.

Experiment 4.7

Testing the Quality of Drinking Water

Materials

✓ clean, transparent pill bottles with tight-fitting caps

✓ samples of the different drinking waters to be tested

✓ pencil and small gummed labels

✓ Ivory liquid hand soap

✓ red cabbage indicator (see Experiment 4.4)

Many people carry bottled water when out of the home. Others drink water in the home that has been filtered through cartridges or purified by under-the-sink systems. Are these better than the local tap water? Some simple tests can be performed at home to help you decide.

Obtain samples of each of the drinking waters that you wish to test, including the local tap water. Each sample should consist of two pill bottles each half-filled with water to be tested. Label each pair so that you can tell them apart from other samples. Copy Table 8 into your science notebook and use it to record your observations. Increase the number of rows in your copy as needed to accommodate your samples. Smell one of the pill bottles of each of the waters. Is the sample entirely transparent? Are there flecks of any material floating in it? Taste it. Write down your observations.

Table 8.
TESTING SAMPLES OF WATER

Source of water sample	Smell	Transparency and color	Taste	Suds	pH

Next, the samples will be tested for hardness. Hard water contains impurities that cause it to need extra soap or detergent to become sudsy. It tends to leave dirt rings around the basin when used for washing clothes. However, there is no evidence that hard water is harmful to drink. To one pill bottle of each of the samples, add one drop of Ivory liquid hand soap. Cap the bottle and shake it vigorously. The fewer suds produced, the harder the water.

Test the pH of the second pill bottle for each sample with red cabbage indicator (see Experiment 4.3). Do all these waters have a pH acceptable for drinking water (6.5–8.5)? How about their other properties? How do they compare? Are you going to use your tap water for drinking? Why or why not? Pour all the tested samples down the drain.

These tests are just a start on testing the quality of the water that you are using. Even so, they may help you to make decisions about whether you wish to continue using the water.

There are other tests that can be performed using water-testing kits that can be purchased from pet stores or pool supply stores.

Science Project Ideas

- Check the pH of as many face soaps as you can. Based on pH, which of the soaps is the mildest for skin use? Which is the harshest? A pH of 7 (neutral) is considered most desirable.

- Examine labels on supermarket products to see which mention pH. List all the products that do. What different types of product are concerned about pH? Why? Pick one or more categories and check the pH against the claims on the label. Report the results and your conclusions.

- What is the pH of the soil in the ground near your house? Does it change when it gets next to the wall of the house? If so, find out why. You will need to mix the soil with about twice as much hot water and allow it to settle. If you cannot get the water clear enough to test, filter it through coffee filter paper in a funnel. If the soil is acid, what is usually added to it to lower the acidity? How does it work?

- What is the optimum pH for a fish tank? Does it depend on whether the fish are freshwater or saltwater fish? What causes pH to change in a fish tank? Show the desirable colors for a particular indicator paper for a fish tank. Discuss how the pH of a fish tank is maintained.

How does acid rain affect plant growth? To simulate acid rain, use one teaspoon of vinegar in two cups of purified water. Adjust the pH of the purified water before use to neutral by adding one or more drops of ammonia or vinegar as needed. Make cuttings of different plants that can live in water, such as philodendron, begonia, coleus, and impatiens. Each cutting should have a healthy leaf and a little stem. Place the stems of the cuttings in neutral water and in acid water and observe the root growth for two to three weeks. Replenish the two kinds of water as needed during the period of observation.

How does acid rain affect metals? Use lemon juice to represent the highly acidic rain that has fallen in this country. Test copper pennies (minted before 1983), aluminum foil, sanded iron nails, and other available metals over a period of several weeks in the liquid. Compare to the same metal standing in purified water. What are the results? What do they show about problems in using these metals?

This book has served as an introduction to the chemistry of water, a vast topic of major importance. The chemical behaviors of water are unique and important in so many ways that only a few of the highlights could be covered here. Hopefully, this book has excited your interest and will serve as a stepping stone to the pursuit of further knowledge of that wondrous chemical, water.

Glossary

acid—A substance that forms hydrogen ions in water.

adhesion (between liquid and solid)—The attraction of a liquid to a solid surface.

atom—The smallest unit that makes up a chemical element.

base—A substance that produces hydroxide ions in water.

boiling point—The temperature at which a liquid begins to boil at normal atmospheric pressure.

bond—The chemical attraction between two atoms that ties them together.

capillary action—The rising of a liquid in a narrow tube.

catalyst—A substance that causes a reaction to speed up without itself undergoing chemical change.

chemical equation—A summary of a chemical change in which formulas are used to show the reactants on the left side of an arrow and the products on the right side.

chemical formula—Shorthand used to show the number and identity of atoms in a unit particle of matter.

chemical reaction—A chemical process by which the identity of at least one substance is changed.

cohesion—The attraction of liquid molecules for each other.

condensation—A change in physical state from a gas to a liquid.

data—Records of observations.

density—The mass of a material divided by its volume.

dissolve—The process by which one material is dispersed uniformly throughout another in units so small as to be invisible.

distillation—The separation of a component of a solution by boiling it out and condensing it back to a liquid.

electrolysis—Using an electric current to break down a compound.

element—A substance that consists of only one type of atom.

enteric—Treated so that it will survive in the stomach but dissolve in the intestines.

evaporation—Escape of molecules from a liquid at temperatures below its boiling point.

freezing point—The temperature at which a liquid changes to a solid.

gas—Matter that has no definite shape or volume.

indicator—A chemical whose color depends on the acidity of the test solution.

insoluble—Not soluble.

liquid—Matter with no definite shape but a definite volume.

metal oxides—Compounds of metals and oxygen.

molecule—The smallest combination of atoms in a neutral substance that has the properties of the substance.

neutralization—The reaction of an acid with a base to eliminate both acidic and basic properties.

neutral solution—A solution that is neither acidic nor basic.

paper chromatography—A method used to separate components of a solution by capillary action on a length of paper.

pH—A measure indicating how acidic or basic a solution is; a pH of 7 is neutral.

physical property—An observable characteristic of a substance.

polar molecule—A molecule within which the electrical charge is unevenly distributed.

retention factor (R_f)—A ratio that describes how far water will carry a chemical up a test strip.

$$\text{retention factor} \quad = \quad \frac{\text{distance the color travels}}{\text{distance the water travels}}$$

saturated solution—A solution into which no more solute will dissolve.

solid—Matter that has a definite shape and a definite volume.

soluble—Able to be dissolved.

solute—Material that dissolves in a solution.

solvent—Material that dissolves a substance.

subscript—The small number at the lower right corner of the symbol for an element in a formula; the subscript stands for the number of atoms of that element in a unit of the compound.

surface tension—A property of liquids in which the surface contracts to the smallest possible area.

Further Reading

Bombaugh, Ruth. *Science Fair Success, Revised and Expanded.* Springfield, N.J.: Enslow Publishers, Inc., 1999.

Bonnet, Bob, and Dan Keen. *Science Fair Projects: Chemistry* New York: Sterling Publishing Co., Inc., 2000.

Gardner, Robert. *Science Projects About Kitchen Chemistry.* Berkeley Heights, N.J.: Enslow Publishers, Inc., 1999.

Martin, Patricia A. Fink. *Rivers and Streams.* Danbury, Conn.: Franklin Watts, 1999.

Wick, Walter. *A Drop of Water.* New York: Scholastic Press, 1997.

Internet Addresses

Granger, Jill. Sweet Briar College. H_2O—*The Mystery, Art, and Science of Water.* ©1999–2002. <http://witcombe.sbc.edu/water/chemistry.html>

U.S. Environmental Protection Agency. Water. 2003. <http://www.epa.gov/water/kids.html>

U.S. Geological Survey. *Water Science for Schools.* 2003. <http://ga.water.usgs.gov/edu>

Index

A

acids, 103–120
    and bases, 109–111
    and red cabbage indicator, 106,
        109–111
    and the hydrogen ion, 106–107
    and pH, 113–117
adhesion, 67
adhesive force, 66–70, 84–86, 91
alcohol, rubbing, 25
atom, 17–18
    hydrogen, 26
    oxygen, 26

B

baking powder, 102
baking soda, 100–102
bases, 103–120
    and acids, 109–111
    and pH, 114–117
    and red cabbage indicator,
        106–117
    and the hydroxide ion, 107
battery, 12, 14
battery cap, 12
boiling point, 51
bond, chemical, 14
bubble, soap, 79–81

C

capillary action, 83–86, 88, 90–91
catalyst, 93, 98
chemical change, 94
chemical equation, 14
chemical formula, 13–14
chemical property, 94
chemical reaction, 15
chemical shorthand, 14
clouds, 32, 54
cohesion, 67
cohesive force, 66–70, 73, 91
condensation, 54
cream of tartar, 100–102

D

data, 6
dissolve, 22–31
distillation, 56–58

E

electrical attraction, 19, 20
electrical charge, 17–18, 19, 20
    and falling water, 18–19
    like charges, 19, 27
    negative, 17, 18
    positive, 17, 18
    unlike charges, 19, 27
electrical repulsion, 19
electrolysis, 14, 94
electron, 17
    charge, 18–20
element, 13
Epsom salts, 24, 58, 74
evaporation, 11, 50–52

F

freezing point, 33, 93

G

gas, 38–39
glass-water interface, 70, 86
graph, 51

H

hydrogen bonds, 40–43, 48–49
    and surface tension, 62
hypothesis, 7

I

ice, 32–35
    colored, 33–34
    density, 39–44
    floating, 39–40, 43–44
    freezing, 46, 48
    melting, 48
    structure, 34–35, 43
indicators, 104–120
    universal, 117
insoluble, 22–24

L

lime, 95
limewater, 96, 109–111
liquid, 38–39
liquid-solid interface, 68–71

M

metal oxides, 95
miscible, 23
molecule, 14
    motion of, 36–41, 48

N

neutral, electrically, 18–20
neutral solution, 109–111
neutralize, acids and bases, 109–111
neutrons, 17
nonpolar, 28
nucleus, 17

O

ocean
    conduct electricity, 16
    salt, 11–12, 16
orbit, 17

P

paper chromatography, 88–92
pH, 113–117, 120
    of household materials, 115–117
pH scale, 114
physical change, 93
polar, 26–28, 40, 48
protons, 17, 26
    charge on, 18

R

rain, 11, 54
raindrops, 72–74
red cabbage indicator, 104–120
retention factor, 90
rubbing alcohol and surface tension, 64

S

safety, 8–10
saturated, 30
science fair display, 6–7

science notebook, 6, 8
scientific process, 7–8
soaps, 75–77, 79–81
solid, 38–39
solubility, 22–31
solvent, 22
states of matter, molecules in, 38–39
static electricity, 20
subscript, 13–14
Super Soaker, 74
surface tension, 59–92
    explanation of, 60–62
    feeling the force of, 64–65

T

theory, 8

V

variable, 7

W

water
    and dissolved table salt, 29–30
    and iron, 98–99
    bent molecule, 14
    boiling, 51
    breakdown by electricity, 13
    chemical formula, 13
    chemical properties, 93–122
    condensation, 53–54
    drops, 66–68, 72, 74
    drinking quality tests, 119–120
    expansion, 41–43
    gas, 52–54
    geological cycle, 11
    hard, 58, 120
    makes reactions possible,
        100–102
    polarity, 26–28, 40, 48, 86
    purified, 10
    reaction with lime, 96–97
    solubility in, 22–25, 29–30, 93
    states of matter, 32–58
    structure, 15
water-candle interface, 70